CHARLES BURCHFIELD

Storm at Sunset, *1959, watercolor, 33" x 55". Courtesy Mr. and Mrs. Harris J. Klein.*

CHARLES BURCHFIELD

BY MATTHEW BAIGELL

WATSON-GUPTILL PUBLICATIONS / NEW YORK

I'd like to express my gratitude to Margit Malmstrom
for her editorial supervision in all its aspects.

First published 1976 in the United States and Canada by Watson-Guptill Publications
a division of Billboard Publications, Inc.
1515 Broadway, New York, N.Y. 10036

Library of Congress Cataloging in Publication Data
Baigell, Matthew.
   Charles Burchfield.
   Includes index.
   1. Burchfield, Charles Ephraim, 1893-1967.
ND237.B89B24   759.13   76-15169
ISBN 0-8230-0533-X

Manufactured in Japan

First Printing, 1976

For Leah and Naomi

ROGUE'S GALLERY, *1916, watercolor, 13 1/2" x 19 5/8". Courtesy Museum of Modern Art, New York, Gift of Abby Aldrich Rockefeller.*

GRAPE ARBOR, *1944, watercolor, 25" x 20". Courtesy Mr. and Mrs. Walter Fillin.*

CONTENTS

COLOR PLATES

INTRODUCTION

An April Mood, *1946–1955, watercolor, 40" x 54". Courtesy Whitney Museum of American Art, New York.*

. . . Burchfield was one of the most religious and passionately realistic artists ever to paint the American landscape . . .

I LIVE IN a mid-Victorian house on a street of comparably aged houses. One has a mansard roof; a few have deep porches; most have projecting window surrounds; all have large trees in front. Whenever I look at the houses and the spaces between, I am reminded of the profound way in which Burchfield understood the small-town, urban landscape.

But Burchfield is known for his rural landscapes as well. I first came to understand this aspect of his work years ago. One April afternoon, roasting a lamb in an Ohio field—the kind that the artist might have hiked through —I looked up at the sky and saw quite distinctly the dark-edged and jagged clouds of *An April Mood*. I saw them through the branches of a tree which had thickened nodes similar to the ones in the painting. The limbs of the tree in the field looked as ugly and distended as those in the painting. I knew, as Burchfield knew, that this would soon change, that the ravaged Good Friday mood would soon give way to the resurrection of life in the spring season. Soon, green leaves and pink flowers would

burst from the enlarged nodes, and the tree would be alive once again.

I realized then that Burchfield was one of the most religious and passionately realistic artists ever to paint the American landscape, and that to see, even for an instant, the landscape through his eyes and mind was an extraordinary experience.

Actually, there are three separate Burchfield landscapes, corresponding to the major phases of his career. These coincide roughly with his youth, his middle years, and his late years. Each, reflecting different but related aspects of his artistic thought, requires our appreciation if we are to understand the full nature of his work. For Burchfield's paintings, unlike those of most other important artists, are difficult to relate to anything but themselves. They do not belong to a particular school and seem to have been little affected by world events. Changes in his attitude coincide with rather than devolve from particular public or political conditions or from those necessities relating alone to the world of art.

In the broad view, there is a

consistency of pattern to his career. Despite the changes in direction, certain themes as well as attitudes remain constant. Most remarkably, the last paintings are very similar to the first ones: in fact, they fulfill the promise of the early works. So involuted was the work of this shy, retiring man, whose life was lived largely within his own mind rather than among people, that any point of entry into his work must of necessity involve the whole of it.[1]

BURCHFIELD'S career does not proceed in a linear progression from its start to its finish, but in a series of small loops within a large triangle. The triangle divides his career into its three principal phases: the youthful landscapes executed until 1917; the paintings use buildings as central themes completed before 1943; and the landscapes finished after 1943. The smaller loops are in constant evidence within and between the dates of the major phases. Burchfield filed his sketches under various headings, by mood, subject, or season, and used them later as notes or as the first roughs of

finished paintings. In occasional watercolors, such as *The Blizzard* (1918–45–63), elements of all three major phases of his career can be seen.

Often, different styles were juxtaposed within a single phase. A painting finished in the early 1960s, for example, but started ten years earlier, might have strokes and dabs typical of the earlier and later developments of this phase in his career. Or, when he worked on or from older sketches or even finished watercolor papers, Burchfield might purposely paint in the older style. On the other hand, he might alter an older work and bring it up to date.

As one can observe in the aging artist the preoccupations of his youth, so the young Burchfield heralds the old man. In attitude as well as in subject matter, the end of Burchfield's career lies close to its origins. To be sure, specific stylistic changes do occur, but only with qualification can one speak of chronology in Burchfield's work.

In the hands of an artist possessing fewer insights into his subject matter, such a limited sphere of activity could easily lead to endless repetition. For Burchfield, however, each new day presented him with new subjects. Seasons and weather patterns changed, and buildings, because they existed on different streets and could be seen at varying times of the day, offering endless variation.

THE BLIZZARD, *1918,*
watercolor, 36" x 54".
Courtesy Mr. and Mrs. Gordon Heald.

LANDSCAPE
OF
CHILDHOOD

DREAM OF A FANTASY FLOWER, *1960–66, watercolor, 33" x 40". Courtesy Mr. and Mrs. John Clancy.*

BURCHFIELD was always unusually responsive to nature. As a child, walking through the woods near his home, he would imagine all sorts of things, creating in his mind's eye feelings of pleasure, terror, fear, or joy.

The landscape was never merely a backdrop for his imaginings, a stage set for childhood fantasies. Early in his life, he came to understand his reciprocal relationship with nature. Nature became a grand force, a living substance capable of dialog with the boy. And as he projected his feelings into nature, he also allowed nature to express its actions and moods through him.

Abnormally sensitive to weather conditions even as a small child, he felt the mysterious forces of nature in their every nuance and change. And growing up in Salem, Ohio, in the Great Lakes –St. Lawrence River weather system, the boy was able to observe a wide variety of conditions—before he was old enough for school he was drawing symbols of weather changes on the family calendar. Although the prevailing winds blow from the southwest to the northeast, the weather patterns of that area are quite volatile. Spring and autumn are as unpredictable as summers are predictably hot and sticky and frequently interrupted by dramatic thunderstorms. In winter, there are many and great snowstorms. Occasionally, the beautiful, destructive phenomenon known as an ice fall will overlay the houses and branches on trees and shrubs with a transparent, reflecting coating of ice. Under a blue sky, trees look like clusters of white diamonds and houses glisten.

In small towns, especially those isolated by surrounding fields, one can see the storms arrive, pass overhead, and depart. One's bodily rhythms respond to the spectacle, and after a severe storm one can find oneself still throbbing with the storm's echo, still participating in the experience.

The young Burchfield must have witnessed many storms as they appeared from the west and southwest and vanished to the north and northeast. In his journals, which he kept throughout his life, he often wrote about his responses to geographical directions, but the north fascinated him most of all. It became a mythical kingdom, a region that still showed its fury after the storm had passed and peace returned to street and backyard. The north, place of action and mystery, mist-shrouded land with darkling forest beyond, haunted Burchfield's imagination throughout his life and became one of the themes he painted over and over.

Just as the normal weather patterns of northern Ohio encouraged his reveries, the landscape itself played a key role in the development of Burchfield's imagination and, ultimately, his art. Whichever artistic, literary, or even musical influences one may want to invoke to describe his paintings, these played a decidedly secondary role to Burchfield's own intimate associations with and observations of the landscape. He painted the landscape felt, heard, and in action.

To a person of Burchfield's sensitivity a casual glance out a window was an intense visual and

MISTY JULY MORNING, *1948, watercolor, 40" x 30 1/2". Courtesy Wells College.*

WOOD LILIES, *1944–62, watercolor, 25″ x 20″. Private collection. Courtesy Frank Rehn Gallery, New York.*

emotional experience, and the landscape he observed each day had a profound effect upon him. Surely, had he lived elsewhere, his art would have evolved differently.

The landscape Burchfield inhabited and painted is a mild one, without conspicuous features. It rolls easily, occasionally interrupting itself with sharp but shallow ravines. Unlike the American West, where vast spaces and enormous mountains overwhelm the viewer; or the Great Plains, where one is made aware of the land itself rather than of what grows upon it; or even the Appalachian ranges closer to Burchfield's home country, where razor-sharp ridges demand attention; the topography of the eastern Great Lakes region blends rather than competes with the plant and insect life living upon it. The topography neither dominates nor is subordinate to the life it supports, but appears to exist in harmony with it, as if a single spirit had united all things. In great measure, Burchfield, through his art, tried to join himself to that spirit.

ONE CAN walk and dream in his landscape—aware of the land, the trees, the forest noises—without being overawed by any of its components. Scaled to the size of man, it is a landscape one can enter and allow one's soul to join while maintaining an inner spiritual equilibrium and a sensitivity to its nuances and larger details.

Although this region, comprising northern Ohio and the western parts of New York and Pennsylvania, offers such joyous, life-affirming experiences, it also possesses, paradoxically, a sustained aura of decay, particularly in its small towns and rural hamlets. Neither old enough to be part of a rooted past nor new enough to be raw and fresh, the communities sag in the landscape. Age seems to have withered the buildings rather than given them an amiable patina.

And industry has scarred the towns badly. Even during Burchfield's lifetime, parts of Ashtabula Harbor, Ohio, his birthplace in 1893; Salem, Ohio, where he lived as a child and youth; and Buffalo, New York, where he settled in 1921, had already become seedy. The river towns along the Ohio and its tributaries, which he visited and painted after 1920—Wellsville, Steubenville, Hammondville— already had the blight, which time has only deepened, upon them. Even their inhabitants seem born grim-faced and not easily given to warming human encounters.

These dual aspects of Burchfield's environment affected his art. He responded intimately to the moods of nature and often saw them as reflections of his own feelings. And the buildings that he painted, rather than being descriptive, evoked whole ranges of human emotion. Few artists have been able to invest trees and houses with such feeling.

Yet, like many people from that part of the country, Burchfield seemed to have lived in a cautious relationship with humanity. Warm and responsive within the comfort of his family, loyal to his few close friends, he was to the public a solitary man, jealously guarding his privacy and uncomfortable without it. He remained in the Buffalo area

THE INTERURBAN LINE, *1920, watercolor, 14 3/4" x 20 3/4". Courtesy Museum of Modern Art, New York, Gift of Abby Aldrich Rockefeller.*

21

CICADA, *1944, watercolor, 30″ x 25″. Courtesy Addison Gallery of American Art, Phillips Academy.*

WALLPAPER DESIGN (SCENIC),
c. 1921–29.
Courtesy the Birge Company.

throughout his adult life rather than move to a more metropolitan community. The world he created there for himself was not simply an adequate one; it was an essential one, necessary for his well-being. He was hardly known even to his neighbors; he could live no other way.

Loath to reveal the amount and quality of the emotion that lay dormant beneath the surface of his pleasant smile, Burchfield sought contact with the world through the tips of his brushes rather than in conviviality. He refused to teach art after he left his position as a wallpaper designer in 1929 even though he could barely support his family during the Depression. It was not until 1949 that he relented, and even then teaching became only a random occupation, done part-time or during summers. He found classroom instruction, like personal contact, too draining on

the energies that he thought should be channeled into his art.

IN HIS journals, he wrote about the fears and pleasures of personal contact, finding crowds and companionship destructive to his work. He linked greatness with spiritual solitude, but he did not consciously seek the latter to ensure the former. Rather, it was as if seclusion were the means by which he could fulfill his expectations of himself.

Burchfield was an artist whose emotions and spontaneous responses were to nature's stimuli rather than to human interactions. His great reservoirs of feeling flowed into an art largely devoid of human relations. Like a great number of characters in novels and stories by Middle Western writers, he directed his energies away from halting and problematic encounters with people. But unlike many such

fictional characters, Burchfield found a personally satisfying way to sublimate his constant, groping desire to express what was deepest within him. Instinctively, he seemed to know that he could express himself with least inhibition by using rural and town landscapes as the conveyors of his feelings.

His communion with his landscape was total and honest. He did not indulge himself in optimistic accounts or fake mythologizing as did painters from more westerly and pioneer-influenced regions, nor did he allow an eastern sophistication to blur his particular vision with esthetic theorizing or flashy brushwork. Rather, he responded to what was most typical of his time and place. Thus, his art not only provides a glimpse of the man's own character but of a particular part of America that existed roughly between 1890 and 1940.

INFLUENCES

BROODING BIRD, *1919–1963, watercolor, 22 1/2" x 29". Courtesy Frank Rehn Gallery, New York.*

. . . life came from the earth; a leaf was more truthful than a diagram.

IN AN ART that was fed so richly from the storehouse of the artist's own imagination and introspection, influences should be considered with qualification. Burchfield read voraciously, particularly in American and Russian literature, and after 1945, in Scandinavian literature. Early in his life he read Eastern mythology. One must assume that although he found accounts of the human situation absorbing, he responded more intimately to descriptions of the landscape, and in Eastern literature, to abstract formulations about nature. Yet whatever he read was probably absorbed in a very special way. His own sensibilities seemed scarcely to be altered and the varying influences that did seep through no doubt reenforced rather than altered his own predispositions.

Burchfield also had a keen regard for music. Bach, Beethoven, and Handel were among his favorites, but Sibelius and Dvořák evidently revealed to him insights that the others could not. The woodland images in their music stimulated him greatly, and he responded profoundly to the suggestions of place, passage of time, and even whole geological eras that it suggested to him. For example, he said that around 1943 reveled in Dvořák's Fourth Symphony, and that its evocation of prehistoric times — the ancientness of the earth, with its outcroppings of rocks — helped generate the forms of *Sun and Rocks* (color plate 32). Despite Burchfield's admiration for the Czech composer, however, it was Sibelius who most impressed him. He felt an unusual rapport with his music and once called him the century's greatest creative genius.

As a child, when not playing in the woods, Burchfield read about them. While still an adolescent, he had read all the works in the Salem Public Library of the naturalist John Burroughs. Perhaps first impressions are the most telling: in any event, there are interesting parallels that may be more than mere coincidence between the careers of both men.

Each was entranced by his own childhood, perhaps even held captive by it, and both preferred to live somewhat apart from the mainstream of ongoing activities. Although Burroughs wrote effectively about all the months of the year, he found a special affinity for late March, especially as it passed into April, the time when the seasons blend and then change. Burchfield, too, found special pleasure in the month of March, even identifying with it. In 1922, for instance, early in his second phase, he said that he wanted to embody March in life and in art. During that month, he also felt an imagined homesickness for the North Country.[2] Its qualities held for him a peculiar electric vibrancy that included images of growth and imminent change. Since a large number of his paintings are of late winter — early spring scenes, it is clear that March, like the North Country, held an important place in his imagination.

NEITHER Burroughs nor Burchfield was a scientific naturalist; both were well-informed poets of nature. To them, nature teemed with life rather than with factual data; it held the promise both of being able to change the mood of man by virtue of its own activities and of creating an atmosphere responsive to his mood.

In an early book, *Wake-Robin* (1871), Burroughs revealed his delight in birds and insects. He described graphically their appearance as well as their chirping and clattering, which he considered to be symbols of the mood and aspect of a particular place. He also observed in certain sounds extensions of his own feelings, finding in the locale, the forest noises, and his own feelings a grand unity of spirit.

Burchfield, too, understood the merging aspects of bird and insect presences in the woods, symbolizing nature's moods as well as his own, and he translated them into sets of visual images.

In one set, birds or insects either key the mood or emphasize it. Such moods range between the emotional and the meteorological. In these paintings, Burchfield both suggested his own feelings through these creatures and chose them to represent weather conditions. As often as not, a gloomy mood coincided with a gray day or an approaching storm, as in *Mysterious Bird,* whereas the first warmth of spring might be represented by two birds singing, as in *March Wind* (color plate 18).

In the other set, he attempted to visualize the sounds he heard in the woods. These became an intimate aspect of his comprehension of nature's totality and were as essential to him as the solid substances of trees and leaves. In fact, they could affect the internal shapes and perimeters of objects. The noises of a woodpecker could vibrate throughout a thicket or infinitely multiply the movements of a tree limb. The drone of katydids and crickets could either augment the sleepiness of a summer's day or prelude the arrival of a summer storm. These paintings reflect the internal moods of the artist even as they help describe the external sounds and conditions of nature.

For, like Burroughs, Burchfield used the appearances and sounds of birds and insects to represent both nature's moods and his own. Where the one ended and the other began was of course unimportant, since it was the suggestion of the merging of the individual's spirit with nature that was the essence of both their work. Those paintings in which woodland sounds are visualized mark one of the significant features of Burchfield's art and are

probably unique in recent painting.

The life forces Burroughs and Burchfield felt in the animate and inanimate objects of nature gave them a way of approaching a fundamental analysis of reality. Their understanding was based on intuition rather than intellect, on experiencing nature over a period of time rather than on abstract philosophical reasoning. They trusted their instincts rather than their intelligence.

THEIR attitudes reveal a direct kinship with the European philosophical movement, Vitalism, and particularly with the ideas of Henri Bergson. Burroughs openly acknowledged the Frenchman's influence, in this country greatest around the turn of the century. Burchfield, if he did not know Bergson's work at first hand, absorbed its tenets through Burroughs.

Like the Vitalists, these Americans understood the concept of life forces instinctively rather than scientifically, and interpreted them with traditional biological and organic metaphors rather than modern mechanical

THE SONG OF THE KATYDIDS ON AN AUGUST MORNING, *1917, watercolor, 17 3/4" x 21 3/4". Courtesy Mr. and Mrs. Meyer P. Potamkin.*

ones. For them, life came from the earth; it was not an achievement of electrical circuits. A leaf was more truthful than a diagram.

In fact, Burroughs and Burchfield opposed the effects that an unchecked scientific development was having on society. Burroughs found that its devastating effect produced an American civilization that was " . . . the ugliest and most materialistic that any country or age ever saw."

And Burchfield wrote at the time he was painting decrepit buildings that he would hate until his last breath " . . . modern industrialism, the deplorable conditions in certain fields such as steel works and mining sections."[3]

Although both deplored modern conditions and the gross insensitivities they engendered, Burchfield, at least, could still find in an industrial scene a redeeming sense of poetry, which if it did not make the prospect pleasant, still allowed it to be reached by the ordinary, humble human mind. He was unimpressed with the power of the steel plants or the energy produced by the coal mines and viewed them rather as deforming presences visited upon land and town. In the end, he responded concretely as a man of the soil rather than abstractly as a man of the city.

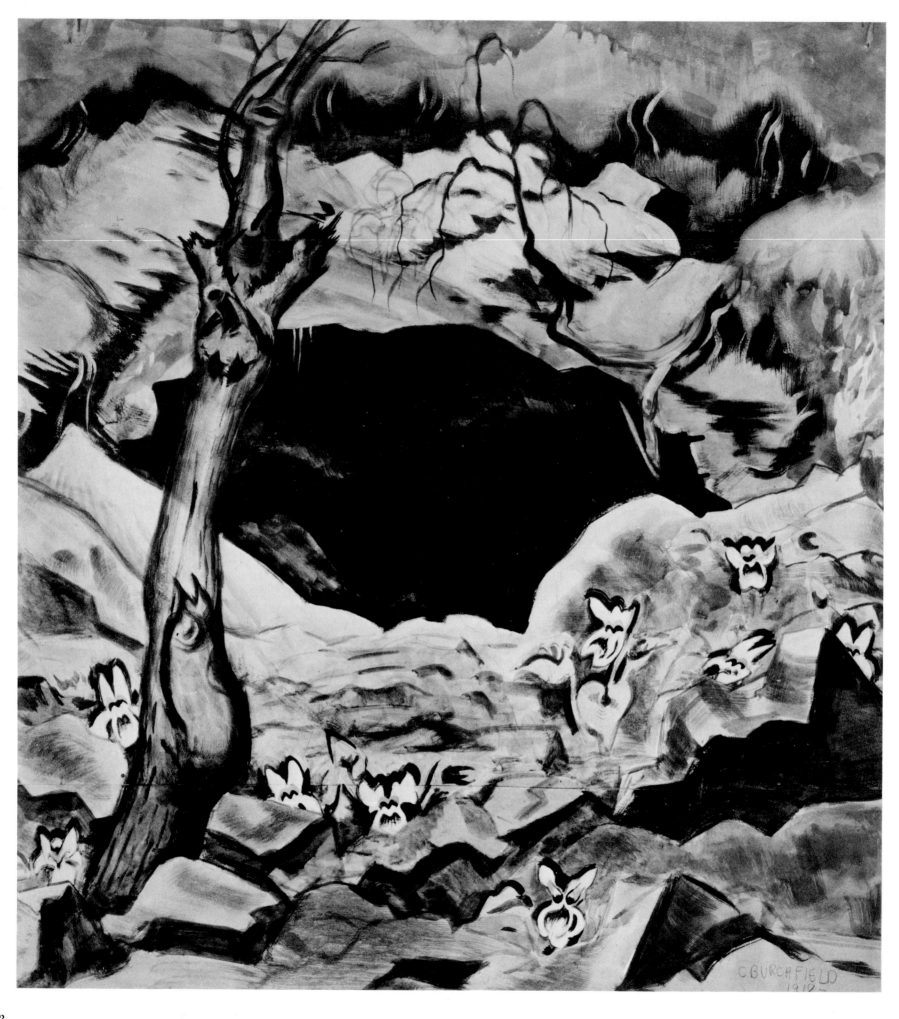

1. TREES AND FIELDS, NOON SUNLIGHT, *1915, watercolor on paper, 14″ x 20″. Courtesy Munson-Williams-Proctor Institute, Edward W. Root Bequest.*

2. SETTING SUN THROUGH THE CATALAPAS, *1916, watercolor on paper, 20-1/4" x 14-1/4"*
Courtesy The Cleveland Museum of Art, Hinman B. Hurlbut Collection.

3. DECORATIVE LANDSCAPE, SHADOW (WILLOWS ON VINE STREET), *1916, watercolor on paper, 19-7/8″ x 13-7/8″.*
Courtesy Munson-Williams-Proctor Institute, Edward W. Root Bequest.

4. DANDELION SEED BALLS AND TREES, *1917, watercolor on paper, 22-1/4" x 18-1/4".*
Courtesy The Metropolitan Museum of Art, A. H. Hearn Fund.

5. CHURCH BELLS RINGING, RAINY WINTER NIGHT, *1917; watercolor on paper, 30" x 19".*
Courtesy The Cleveland Museum of Art, Gift of Mrs. Louise M. Dunn.

6. GARDEN OF MEMORIES, *1917, crayon and watercolor on paper, 25-3/4″ x 22-1/2″.*
Courtesy The Museum of Modern Art, New York, Gift of Abby Aldrich Rockefeller.

7. STARLIT WOODS, *1917, watercolor on paper, 33-1/2" x 22-1/2".*
Courtesy Dr. and Mrs. Coleman Mopper, Huntington Woods, Mich.

8. THE NIGHT WIND, *1918, watercolor and gouache on paper, 21-1/2" x 21-7/8".*
Courtesy The Museum of Modern Art, New York, Gift of A. Conger Goodyear.

9. ABANDONED COKE OVENS, *1918, watercolor on paper, 21-1/2" x 35". Courtesy Wichita Art Museum, Wichita, Kansas.*

10. SPRING TWILIGHT, *1920, watercolor on paper, 20-1/4" x 26-1/4". Courtesy Mr. and Mrs. Mortimer Spiller, Buffalo, New York.*

11. HOUSES, *1920, watercolor on paper, 12" x 17-1/2". Courtesy Mr. and Mrs. Walter Fillin, Rockville Centre, New York.*

12. COAL MINE—END OF THE DAY, *1920, watercolor on paper, 18" x 31". Courtesy Frances and L. D. Cohen.*

13. Winter Solstice, *1920–21, watercolor on paper, 21-1/2" x 35-1/2". Courtesy Columbus Gallery of Fine Arts, Ferdinand Howald Collection.*

14. SULPHUROUS EVENING, *1922–29, watercolor and pencil on board, mounted on paper, 24" x 30". Courtesy The St. Louis Art Museum, Eliza McMillan Fund.*

15. RED BIRDS AND BEECH TREES, *1924. Courtesy of Mr. and Mrs. Mortimer Spiller, Buffalo, New York.*

16. Hilltop at High Noon, *1925, oil on board, 31" x 22". Courtesy The Pennsylvania Academy of the Fine Arts.*

A Little Cabin, *1918, watercolor, 9" x 12". Courtesy Burchfield Family.*

THE ART STUDENT

BARREN TREES, *1914, watercolor, 13 1/4" x 9 1/2". Courtesy Mr. Stantly Malzman.*

...the director called him a genius, an artist in advance of his time.

TO YOUNG and aspiring painters, art school can be an illuminating revelation or it can create a hurdle that they spend the remainder of their lives trying to pass beyond. Fortunately, the Cleveland School of Art (now the Cleveland Institute of Art) afforded Burchfield a pleasant and generally useful set of experiences. He studied there from 1912 to 1916.

Although a provincial school, its faculty introduced Burchfield to a variety of styles. He evidently responded to the more exotic ones. These included Art Nouveau illustrations as well as Chinese and Japanese prints. Although he was aware of the Swiss modernist Ferdinand Hodler, by 1916 he had surprisingly little exposure to contemporary European movements. The major influences upon the formation of his personal manner were a modern decorative style, Far Eastern art, and traditional Western modes.

The most important and probably most sensitive of his teachers, Henry G. Keller, about whom Burchfield often commented later in life, seemed to understand his strengths most fully. At least he encouraged their development. Perhaps his own strengths were similar to those of his pupil, for in recognizing and commenting upon Burchfield's genius for pattern, rather than the creation of solid form, he described his own art as well.

It was Keller's attitude toward art that was probably most useful to Burchfield's development. His purpose in looking at the works of others was to discover in them means to liberate his own individual responses, not to imitate them. Such an approach permitted him to define his own character and personality, and to be able to find in other artists those aspects that would expand his own outlook. A difficult synthesis at best, its success could lead to an art style and range of subject matter honestly reflective of his being, a style of genuine individual integrity; or, in failure, it could lead to an endless quest for self-realization through a series of imitative, readymade formulas supplied by others.

Perhaps Burchfield's innocence of contemporary European trends was a blessing in regard to Keller's teaching. The younger man certainly arrived at an individual style early in his career. By contrast, individualism, an important and ever-present thread in American painting in those years, often foundered after artists were "liberated" by Parisian styles and began to imitate one or another major figure.

BURCHFIELD'S impulse to develop his own style and individuality was recognized and encouraged by his teachers. During an exhibition held at the School in 1917, a year after he graduated, the director called him a genius, an artist in advance of his time. Keller himself pointed out the very modern combination of tactile, auditory, and occasional gustatory sensations that were evoked by his watercolors.[4] Partly hyperbole, these comments nevertheless indicate the reassurance Burchfield must have received in Cleveland despite the very untraditional look of his early efforts (color plate 1).

The significance of the Chinese and Japanese art which he had seen and the Hindu and Buddhist mythology which he had read by 1915 is difficult to

SUNFLOWER, *Henry G. Keller, c. 1914–15, watercolor on cardboard, 19 7/8" x 14".*
Courtesy Cleveland Museum of Art, Anonymous Gift.

EARLY SPRING WEATHER, *Henry G. Keller, before 1915, watercolor on masonite, 19 1/8″ x 14 1/8″.*
Courtesy Cleveland Museum of Art, Gift of Mrs. Arthur L. Brockway.

assess. We do not know what, specifically, he had read or how much he understood, but he did indicate that the idea of personifying natural phenomena particularly excited him. No doubt, it reenforced the passages he remembered in Burroughs' writings in which wildlife symbolized nature's moods.

There is no question that Chinese and Japanese art offered stylistic cues to the young student and helped provide him with an attitude toward subject matter that he retained until his death. These art forms, too, could have reminded him of passages in Burroughs.

Specifically, Burchfield often said that an exhibition of Chinese scroll paintings seen in 1914 stimulated him to execute, in continuous form, "all-day sketches." These works would include sunrises, mid-morning clouds, afternoon thunderstorms, sunsets, and moonrises.

He began to collect "all-day sketches" soon after the exhibition and he determined to realize them by formulating a set of conventions based on nature. His efforts, as he subsequently realized, were premature. He did not yet have the technical facility to complete them. It was not until 1943 that such paintings emerged in recognizable form

EARLY AUTUMN, *Ch'ien Hsüan, 13th century, ink and colors, 10 1/2" x 47 1/4". Courtesy The Detroit Institute of Arts, Purchase General Membership and Donations Fund.*

(color plate 26).

His plan of making all-day sketches indicated an immediate and profound appreciation of Eastern, especially Chinese, art. Burchfield must have intuitively understood the connection between his own ramblings in the woods and the Chinese scroll paintings. They provoked a series of delayed responses throughout his career, so that, like other events of his youth, this early exhibition was a continuing influence on him.

Like a Chinese artist, Burchfield wanted to feel the harmony of the universe by communing with all things. Evidently, he felt that each object had its special soul, and this he tried to reveal in its various guises and moods.

As in the concept of the Tao, which informs much Chinese painting, Burchfield felt a unified power permeating the entire universe, so that spirit and matter existed as one. In a grove of trees, he once expressed these complex thoughts easily. "I am home again—this is mine . . . . Here only can I be with God; the spirit coming through these trees is both me and my creator, merged."[5]

He found divine reality in the beauty of the world, and when he felt as one with the landscape he

was moved to tears. Such moments of recognition happen only by mysterious processes of thought and feeling, difficult to define. There are, for example, those days when a person while walking in the woods concentrates on his own feelings and is at ease with them. There are other days when one is not aware of himself as much as he is of the rightness of a particular landscape setting, where each individual rock or leaf seems to be ripe with meaning and responsiveness.

The finest days, the ones approximating both the concept of the Tao as well as the mood qualities Burchfield wanted to project into a painting, are those in which one is aware both of himself and of the landscape setting and in which one can feel both aspects—his own being and the beingness of the landscape—gloriously burgeoning and mingling within himself. There are recurrent feelings of expansiveness and of tremendous humility, both states of mind recorded by Burchfield in his journals. At times, he wept: at other moments, he might, as in the genesis of the painting *Oncoming Spring*, walk

in the woods, find himself in a howling storm and feel the need to paint for ". . . a few glorious hours when I seemed to become part of the elements." (color plate 35).[6]

In such incantatory moments of oneness with nature, a painting like *Oncoming Spring* ". . . seemed as if it [had] materialized under its own power." For Burchfield, these must have been the perfect moments of his life, literally beyond words and very personal in meaning. He must have sensed the duality of his existence separate from nature and at the same time his spirit at one with nature.

IT IS NOT surprising that Burchfield's sense of composition is related to composition in Chinese art. His forms, more in his first and third phases than in his second, suggest the possibility of growth. They, too, do not always resolve themselves into tightly structured compositions; they suggest not the frozen moment, captured since the Renaissance in European art, but instead the experience of time, duration, and infinity characteristic of Eastern art.

Such comparisons with Eastern art should not be pushed too far, since Burchfield's paintings remained Western, even typically American, in their multiplication of detail. Rather than simplifying and bringing out essential characteristics, he piled motif upon motif. Instead of there being a continuous line between himself and the universe, it seemed as often as not that a collision had taken place. Nature did not flow through him, as much as he sometimes actively tried to meet it and gather it in.

It was as if he walked in a field and concentrated on that particular element which struck his fancy first. Then he would turn his attention to the next object and try to record both, separately and simultaneously. On balance, his was a participatory landscape rather than a reflective one, a landscape of immediate feeling rather than contemplation.

At least one similarity between Burchfield's art and Chinese painting does merit further notice. It appears in both his paintings and drawings and can be seen most easily in black-and-white reproductions. On the tonal, or value, scale of dark to

57

light, or black to white, where the darker the value the more black there is in the pigment mixture (dark green, dark red, etc.) and the lighter the value the more white there is in the mixture (light green, etc.), Burchfield often clustered the values around four different and distinct tones. Of the infinite number of possibilities of value in any painting, he usually employed only four — very dark, medium dark, medium light, and very nearly white.

This characteristic appears quite obviously in *Springtime in the Pool*, a painting otherwise not Chinese in feeling. In other works, where fragments of dark-value trees wander across the pic- ture plane, while abruptly contrasting light-value forms suggest deep spaces, both the value system and the compositional form are more reminiscent of Chinese painting.

Again, such a technical (as opposed to conceptual) relationship with Chinese art should not be overly emphasized, because the four-value system might have been learned from one of the art teachers in Cleveland.

Even though Burchfield had not become familiar with Parisian modernism during his student years, his style revealed an extremely advanced sensibility. His flattened forms were not modeled with realistic highlights and shadows. Their colors were bright and unmodulated. Edges of forms were simplified, turning recognizable images into abstract patterns. Contours, rather than a sense of weight or gravity, defined objects. Two or three bands of color placed one above the other indicated a tree trunk, a device used by Matisse and Derain in the first years of the century and perhaps independently discovered by Burchfield (color plate 1).

The relative sizes of objects follow no logical order. Forms normally read as part of distant skies appear to float in front of trees. Colors that one expects to grow soft instead stiffen and become harsh. Shapes that should diminish in size seem to blossom before our eyes.

POPLAR WALK, *1916, watercolor, 19 7/8" x 19 7/8". Courtesy Munson-Williams-Proctor Institute, Edward W. Root Bequest.*

THE FIRST PHASE

1915
——————————
1918

BACK TO THE WOODS

SNOWSTORM IN THE WOODS, *1917, watercolor, 20" x 42". Courtesy The Art Institute of Chicago, Gift of Mr. Clay Bartlett.*

. . . each sensation appeared fresh and new, as if he were the first person on earth.

BY 1915, Burchfield began to tire of the routine nature of art classes and of the time wasted studying life drawing. He no longer found living in the city very attractive either, preferring to be home in Salem, hiking through the countryside. He especially missed the view from his bedroom window. Here was, for Burchfield, " . . . the entrance to a romantic land."[7] Here was the point from which he knew his art would spring to life.

He firmly believed that the ideas which were to haunt him for his entire adult life were generated in 1915 as well. He felt that the ideas of a lifetime's effort had to be gathered and tested then or never at all. Although he still had a year remaining at art school, he always said that his career as an artist really began in that year, 1915.

He decided at that time that he had to extract his means of visualization and his motivating concepts directly from nature rather than from classroom procedures. In voluminous studies and sketches made that year, he sought ways to record the multiple levels on which he perceived nature.

It was also by a series of personal ventures that he dated his career as an artist. The "all-day sketches" were begun. In addition, he considered the possibility of colors creating their own particular sounds. Within a short time, this led him to speculate about the sounds particular objects might make, such as railroad tracks, or the type of music twisting tree bark might suggest, and, ultimately, to the visualization of insect and bird sounds. He also wanted to formulate a set of conventions based on nature. These never evolved, but they did help provoke the conventionalizations of mood that appeared in his work in 1917 and again after 1943.

To be able to work quickly, to be able to gather and test all those ideas, Burchfield standardized his palette, limiting himself to twelve colors, in addition to black and white. Particular colors, whatever their symbolic value, also denoted specific objects. Sunlit earth was orange, grass appeared yellow, and shadows were cast in red-violet.

In short, he was trying to find specific ways to respond to and reproduce all that he felt, saw,

and heard in nature. For a twenty-two-year-old man studying art in a provincial center which still lacked a museum, this was not merely youthful enthusiasm, but an early indication of a way of thinking and feeling that characterized the greater part of his career.

In fact, the paintings of 1915 and 1916 contain many themes Burchfield often used later: suns and moons behind trees, intimate foliage studies, forest path and wider roadway views, day and evening scenes, and stormy and calm views. Certain motifs recurred in different guises and seemed to have special meaning for him. The idea of north has already been mentioned. The path into the woods could suggest desolation, death, or spring growth by the length of the brush strokes, their variations in thickness, and their repetition (color plate 27).

Burchfield also painted particular plants whose forms intrigued him, including Queen Anne's lace and the dandelion. The latter he held in particular esteem, painting it in day and night scenes, from bird's-eye and worm's-eye views, at arm's length or as part of a larger composition. Once, he was moved to say, "God's greatest gift to me is the ability to be astonished anew each year by the almost incredible beauty of a dandelion plant in full bloom."[8]

HIS ABILITY to find so much pleasure in a mere weed reflects Burchfield's approach to his work. Not the subject itself, but the conception of the subject in the mind of the artist was sufficient for the production of great art.[9] To him, the dandelion was not a weed at all, but a fantastical plant that lived in dialog with the forest or the moon or the night creatures. So thoroughly did the plant engage his imagination that it served as the principal subject for two of the most fully realized paintings from the first and last phases of his career (color plates 4 and 44).

The most theatrical of all the motifs Burchfield favored were those we may call the apocalyptic views in which he seemed to be celebrating the very existence of the earth itself (color plate 16). Realistic during the 1920s and 1930s, later in his career they projected an intense religiosity, as the sun or the moon reached out to touch the earth. In fact, *Hot September Wind* suggests as few twentieth-century paintings, the presence of the Diety in nature, a presence Burchfield consciously sought as he grew older.[10] Not since the days of the Hudson River School painters in the mid-nineteenth century had an American painter so obviously commemorated the religious aspects of the landscape and so thoroughly rejoiced in doing so.

Whatever the theme, Burchfield preferred interpreting it within an intimate landscape. Not surprisingly, he found the ravine of the Genesee River in western New York, 350 feet deep, too overwhelming in size to render agreeably. In his desire to become immediately familiar with a landscape scene and to paint it on a small scale, he parted company with the Hudson River School painters and revealed affinities with artists such as Washington Aliston, George Inness, and Albert Pinkham Ryder. They, too, felt mysterious forces emanating from nature and

HOT SEPTEMBER WIND, *1953,*
watercolor, 39" x 29".
Courtesy Kennedy Gallery, New York.

responded to them in an intimate way. But, unlike their land-scapes, Burchfield's are not brooding ones. It would be easy to say, therefore, that the congruent feelings of affirmation, religiosity, and intimacy noted in Burchfield's paintings draw on different traditions in American art, but it is more than likely that in Cleveland Burchfield learned little of the traditions of American art. Rather, his paintings suggest the fulfillment of his own needs before nature; any connection with the past is really a product of the viewer's hindsight.

Burchfield carried little ideological or historical baggage when he went into the woods. He traveled instead with a fresh sense of adventure. As a young man, he wanted to mingle old sensations of childhood with the ones he was then experiencing. He once commented that he wanted to spend every moment absorbing the sights about him. At times, each sensation appeared fresh and new, as if he were the first person on earth.

His need to be with nature was essential, and the joys of hiking never ceased. After an illness in the late 1950s, he bemoaned the fact that he could no longer tramp through the woods of a winter's evening after a snowstorm.

A single tree could with minimal coaxing transform itself endlessly before his eyes. Depending on the season, the time of day, and the weather conditions, its colors, patterns, and moods multiplied in infinite extension. In late autumn, the few remaining leaves, when seen looking straight up at the sky, wove a loose tapestry with the branches; after a storm, the bark, blackened by rainwater, slowly turned gray as it dried. In winter, the tree's branches formed intricate stained-glass traceries against the northern sky, with its ambiguous suggestions of far-off times and places. In winter sunlight the sharp shadows of one branch on another seemed to multiply the number of limbs, an effect Burchfield captured with long, black whiplash lines. In spring, the same tree trembled with newly formed leaves. After an early summer shower the tree grew majestic when, still in shadow, it was surrounded and silhouetted by shafts of sunlight breaking through the scattering clouds. And following a heavy summer storm, a time that Burchfield loved, the tree might seem to dissolve and blend upward into the mist.

EACH OF the moods assumed by the tree suggested a corresponding mood in Burchfield, so that in recording the one he invariably recorded the other. Mood and mystery, affirmation and joy, became as much a part of the tree as its leaves, branches, and trunk. In this way, Burchfield could suggest the accord he desired between himself and nature as well as between particular objects and the entire landscape. A common spirit pervaded all.

No wonder he often felt moments of despair and exhilaration before the epic power of nature, and no doubt he would have agreed with Rodin when the sculptor said, " . . . the artist, full of feeling, can imagine nothing that is not endowed like himself. He suspects in nature a great consciousness like his own. There is not a living organism, not an inert object, not a cloud in the sky, not a green shoot in the meadow, which does not hold for him the secret of the great power hidden

in all things."[11]

Burchfield's need to be in constant communion with nature, even during his middle phase, helps explain his almost compulsive habit of drawing and sketching outdoors. He considered his sketches in relation to his watercolors as chamber music to symphonies, capable of revealing intimacies and insights the larger works were unable to capture. They also allowed a kind of daydreaming with pen or pencil that brushes and full palette did not permit. And a drawing could, as he once indicated, continue the afterglow of creativity when done without the responsibility of major effort after the completion of a watercolor.

More practically, drawings also allowed compositional problems to be arbitrated. Since Burchfield often painted in the studio behind his house (after he moved to Buffalo), drawings would keep a view of a mood fresh. If he chose to return to a sketch months or even years later, it could rekindle a host of associations approximating the original sensations. Or, in the interaction between remembered and new emotions, additional ideas might begin to take hold. Far from being ancillary to his main efforts, drawing served a variety of operative and imaginative purposes integral to Burchfield's efforts.

NOSTALGIA
FOR
CHILDHOOD

WOMAN IN A DOORWAY, *1917, tempera on mounted cloth, 24" x 30". Courtesy Phillips Collection, Washington, D.C.*

STREET SCENE IN NEW YORK, *1916*,
pencil, 11 1/2" x 8 1/2".
Courtesy Frank Rehn Gallery, New York.

IN OCTOBER, 1916, after graduating from art school, and having completed about 150 paintings, Burchfield traveled to New York City to study at the National Academy of Design. He spent one day attending classes, lingered about a month in the city, and returned home depressed and feeling as if he were a failure. Immediately, he took a sketching walk in the snow, heard the wind in the trees, and decided that the music he heard there was far superior to city sounds.

It is not surprising that he left New York so quickly. In place of trees, there were people; instead of solitude, there were crowds. A solitary dreamer, he did not care to celebrate either the city's human activity or its kaleidoscopic frenzy as other artists, both experimental and traditional, had done. Nor did he choose to contest the city and to find in it elements of alienation as did such German Expressionists as Ludwig Kirchner. Yet Burchfield's one known view of New York, a drawing, is similar to studies made by Kirchner and, before him, by the Norwegian, Edvard Munch. People appear as

automatons, overwhelmed both by the impersonality of the buildings and by the disappearance of human relationships.

The city was certainly not the type of landscape Burchfield favored. His flight from it reaffirmed his artistic inclinations which, contrary to those of most important twentieth-century artists, would never flourish in cosmopolitan centers.

Because he had to let an environment soak into his system before he could feel responsive to it, Burchfield was an unenthusiastic traveler. Even in his mature years, he was often reluctant to leave his home for very long. Although he moved to Buffalo in 1921, he said that many years passed before he had weaned himself from Ohio. And once, in 1955, when a friend and patron invited him to the city in which the patron lived to create a series of paintings, Burchfield rejected the idea because he never took sketching trips away from his

familiar haunts. "I have to live for some time in a place before I can begin producing genuine expressions of my reactions to the place," he said.[12]

Furthermore, if he were to admit a new range of potential subjects to his normal repertoire, he would let them simmer in his mind for several years before exploring them further. Such selectivity did not imply a lack of adventure or a conservative cast of mind as much as it indicated an intensity of commitment to a chosen subject, not easily lavished on casual visits or momentary scenes.

The quick return from New York City in 1916 also allowed Burchfield entrance to that romantic land seen from his bedroom window. No mere literary conceit, the phrase aptly describes his state of mind then, for in the immediately succeeding months he indulged an acute nostalgia for childhood memories, feelings, and images. Boyhood reminiscenses filled his mind as he tried to resurrect the impressions of his earliest years. The woods became a fearsome place once again; a cricket's rasp in the sunlight could set off a host of

childhood associations. His art became a kind of remembrance of things past. It was a period of marking time for the twenty-four-year-old artist; he was not yet ready to enter the adult world, nor was he willing to give up his youth.

BURCHFIELD'S infatuation with his childhood, a recurring phenomenon for him, lasted through 1917. In fact, he termed that year his golden year, as he delved further into his memories. It was a happy time; he was protected and secure in his environment and enjoyed the freedom to paint as he wished.

These early years were very important to Burchfield. Each one added new dimensions to his thinking and his facility as an artist. He subsequently thought so much of those first years of artistic self-definition that he considered 1915, 1916, 1917, and 1918 as individual periods in his life. The many remaining years of his career he lumped together by decades or stylistic phases. No single year after 1920, it seems, equaled the in-

tensity of feeling or of remembrance of the early ones.

In 1917, he worked like one possessed. By the end of that year, he had painted around 400 of the roughly 4,000 works attributed to him. Among the 400, there were some false starts, some incompleted works, as well as a number of rough sketches. Compared to the earlier paintings, his style was already changing.

He relied less on flat patterning as the months progressed, and he developed a more supple brushstroke. This developed in part from using a different kind of brush, one which allowed thicker strokes. It became no longer necessary to outline and then fill in: Burchfield could "draw" more easily with color.

The new brush, first used either just before or just after the trip to New York City, allowed strokes to swirl independently of objects. Spatial recessions could grow more fluid, and simple forms might lose their borders. But, more important, it let Burchfield use the stroke more easily as a conveyor of mood. He could activate the entire picture

surface and allow the sky or trees to vibrate in harmony with other forms. For the first time, in 1917, the sky began to be used as an effective part of his compositions rather than as a mere backdrop. Skies grew rich in color and texture, and developed patterns of their own apart from those created by plant and insect forms imposed upon them.

Once Burchfield perceived that line and shape need not be tied to flat patterning or object definition, he was able to explore further and give visual form to two ideas that had earlier intrigued him—the visualization of sound and the conventionalization of mood.

INSECT noises began to appear with frequency in paintings of 1917 as thin, calligraphic strokes that insinuated a monotonous hum. They seemed, when combined with envisaged heat waves, to saturate a painting not only with suggestions of sounds but with the sense of a steaming summer's day. The repetitive strokes, energizing leaves and grass, re-

SONG OF THE WOOD THRUSH, *1949–65, watercolor, 33" x 40". Courtesy Dr. and Mrs. Eugene L. Gottleib.*

call those extenuated, meditative observations most of us have made of a single blade of grass or of an individual leaf which quivered imperceptibly, but palpably.

The conventionalization of mood suggested more difficult problems, but offered richer solutions, both compositional and spiritual. Different feelings became associated in Burchfield's mind with specific designs. These forms, indicating emotional states, grew as a parallel idea to the notion he held in 1915 of shaping a set of conventions based on nature's forms. Begun, in part, as shorthand notations to save time, they came to dominate many paintings, serving as mood conditioners as well as formal devices to link together sections of a watercolor. A unique achievement in modern American painting, this very personal vocabulary reappeared in Burchfield's work after 1943 when he returned to the landscape themes of his youth.

He devised about twenty notations which he called "Conventions for Abstract Thoughts." These depicted, rather unexpect-

edly in one so at home with nature, a gamut of negative feelings ranging from melancholy and madness to evil, morbidity, and menace.

Reveling in childhood memories at this time, the conventions no doubt helped Burchfield recall the moods, and probably the fears, of his youth. In his journals of that period, he referred to the awfulness of the black north and to the wild winds which came from the southwest. A day could become an evil thing and sounds could ring alarmingly in the woods, even though the grown man knew there was only silence. Terror replaced elation as faces appeared in trees.

In *The Night Wind* (color plate 8), a work of 1918, whose cutout shapes recall the manner of 1916, a variety of conventions abound. The spiral hooks of the wind crossing the sky indicate fear. Melancholy appears as the rising humplike forms of the dark cloud in the middle left. Out of the distant tree forms rise the sightless eyes of insanity, while in the foreground the saddle-shaped windowtops, suggesting morbidity, are surrounded by

further circles of insanity. This is not a simple recording of a night wind, but a child's grim fantasy of the rural dark, where vision is minimal, sound maximal, and terror overwhelming. Burchfield had created the conventions to symbolize the various memories and images of his earliest years.

The conventions often had a source in specific imagery. A variety of designs can be imagined in the gingerbread carving of Victorian front doors as well as eave ornaments. Glass panes may be circular, oval, or diagonal. Night patterns of moving clouds and the bright moon suggest shockingly strange images, which, with only slight alteration, Burchfield indicated in the sky of *The Night Wind* as fear.

Though fanciful, the conventions were also factual, and to Burchfield they must have held additional meanings, recalling particular doorways, houses, evenings, or incidents. Yet the forms are neither arch nor arcane, for they allow a viewer the chance to explore his own fantasies and remembrances. They invoke the nightmares of childhood in all of us.

FLIGHT OF BLACKBIRDS AT DAWN, *1916, watercolor, 14" x 20". Courtesy Mr. and Mrs. William Hayes Bender, Jr.*

These paintings project a sensibility less concerned with problems of pictorial organization than with evocation of mood. Burchfield's work, then, seems more an extension of his personality, synthesizing present and past images, than an objective creation divorced from his feelings. For these reasons, his paintings, which honor the modern shibboleths of relative spacelessness, disruptive perspectives, arbitrary color handling, minimal modeling, and raw application of watercolor pigment, do not look like paintings by other modern artists. One feels that Burchfield is more concerned with responding to a tree than with the manipulation of green or brown paint. His friend and dealer, Frank Rehn, once observed in similar fashion, "He's one of the few artists I know who doesn't talk about his technique. All he's interested in is whether or not he has created the mood he felt at the time of painting the picture."[13]

Many people spend their lives looking backward at some hallowed moment of their youth and cast their present existence in its image. Burchfield might well have done this in 1917, letting a range of memories and images stand for that moment. He could manipulate his past in an agreeable manner and he could have begun quite easily to imitate himself. But his new responses to his environment created new imagery and new sensations. He could not force the old ones over and over. By the end of 1917, or in the first month or two of 1918, the magic of recollecting childhood memories had evaporated. He felt that he had sufficiently probed his past and exhausted, for the moment, its personal and artistic possibilities; he found that it no longer served as a source of specific imagery.

NOONTIDE IN LATE MAY, *1917,*
watercolor and gouache, 21 3/8" x 17 3/8".
Courtesy Whitney Museum of American Art, New York.

POPLARS IN JUNE, *1917, watercolor, 18" x 22". Courtesy Mr. Ralph Wilson.*

ICE GLARE, *1933, watercolor on mounted paper, 30 3/4" x 24 3/4". Courtesy Whitney Museum of American Art, New York.*

84

THE SECOND PHASE
1918
1943

THE "HAUNTED" HOUSES

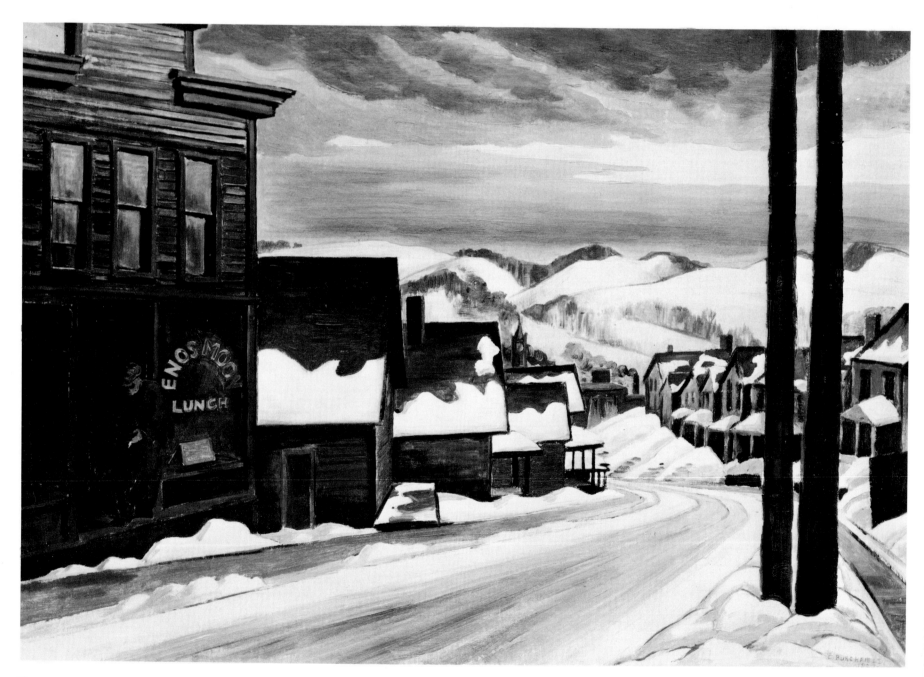

WINTER, EAST LIVERPOOL, *1927, oil on canvas, 22" x 32". Courtesy Albright-Knox Art Gallery, Buffalo.*

. . . these buildings, with their staring, frightened eyes, have the look of going mad with loneliness.

IN 1917 Burchfield began to turn his attention, as he later stated, from nature to humanity. But it was, in fact, a humanity largely devoid of people: rather, it was populated by houses. For the shy young artist, they became surrogates for humanity and, like the landscapes that he still painted, extensions of his own feelings.

By mid-year, houses had largely taken the place of trees in Burchfield's imagination. Where he had found poetry in a branch, he now discovered a new grace in a window, a chimney, or a gable. If he no longer read his childhood memories so obviously into the buildings, he did maintain in the realization of their facades a similar range of feeling. He found in them the look of evil or astonishment, a brooding, perhaps a carnivorous, quality. He saw in them a silent expectancy, a capacity for feeling as if they had achieved the same degree of organic development possessed by leaves and wind-blown clouds.

Tramping the streets of Salem, he saw the houses as symbols of the lives they sheltered. Since he undoubtedly knew the inhabitants of many of them, the paintings offered a way of studying people without having to touch them in any way or disturb his own thoughts about them. These paintings, therefore, became a very personal series of comments, largely melancholic in general observation, about the town he lived in.

Because of their intimate qualities, these houses are not yet the tired, rundown buildings Burchfield began to paint in quantity around 1920 and afterward. Many of the houses of 1917–1919 have instead the same spooked look about them that evokes comparison with *The Night Wind* (color plate 8). They seem to share a common sense of gloom and fear.

In a striking observation made when some of these works were shown in New York City in 1920, the art critic of *The New York Times* said that these buildings, with their staring, frightened eyes, have the look of going mad with loneliness.[14] Perhaps Burchfield himself, caught between his past and his present, also felt as if he were going mad with loneliness. The subsequent events of his life tell us that these paintings do not represent anything quite as dramatic as impending insanity, but they may reflect one of those moments of intense despair that periodically gripped Burchfield and may help account for the wellspring of feeling in his work that seems to reach beyond gloom to neurotic dejection.

AS A GROUP, the strange and haunting houses of 1917–1919 reach for a nerve that could only be found in the silence of that lonely bedroom which no longer gave happy access to the land of romance. In trying "to express the ingrown lives of solitary people," as he said, the buildings, tissue-paper thin, are vehicles for Burchfield's state of mind rather than realistic observations of Middle Western architecture. Nevertheless, like the strange forms in the landscape paintings, these buildings, too, are based on fact, not fancy. With their heavy overhangs giving their twin upper windows a tawdry, mascaraed look and their open-mouthed, twin- and tri-columned porches, these houses

FROSTED WINDOWS, *1917, watercolor, 25 1/2" x 19 1/2". Courtesy Mr. and Mrs. Clyde B. Hurtt Kirkwood.*

POPLAR TREE AND HOUSE, *1917, watercolor, 20″ x 14″. Courtesy Dr. and Mrs. Frederick Mebel.*

are standard Ohio types and can still be seen on virtually every lowerclass and middleclass street in the state.

Burchfield disclosed an interest in miners at this time and in a few paintings recorded their difficult conditions. But ever the fantasist, he found their abandoned huts, the coke ovens, and mines more fascinating. Plentiful around Salem, they were all left to decay when deserted. The crumbling huts and ovens, as they discolored, and the mine openings clogged with vegetation, suggested prehistoric feelings to Burchfield, as if they had been discarded centuries earlier. One oven suggested the form of a buzzard. Another had growing near it horsetails, a plant that had existed during the Age of Vegetation in which coal was formed (color plate 9). But this interesting development, adding geological to the biological components he used, was cut short by his induction into the army and his service in South Carolina in a camouflage unit.

Although Burchfield did not seem to find the experience a bad one, he returned to Salem in

January, 1919, and began to suffer a period of depression, despair, and doubt. The changes in locale, to which he often had difficulty adjusting, probably contributed to his bleak mood. Possibly the smug provincialism and patriotism he found in Salem also offended him. So great had the anti-German hysteria become that a hotel in town refused to serve German-fried potatoes, and its chef rechristened sauerkraut "cabbage salad." The recognition of such destructive sentiments among his fellow townsmen helped stimulate the penetrating glimpses of small-town American life that soon followed.

In the paintings done immediately after his homecoming, he became obsessed with expressing the feelings of birds. He sketched landscapes as they might appear to a bird, or he made studies of a nest in which a mother bird might cradle her young. As buildings had served as repositories for his intense loneliness before his tour of duty, now birds functioned in the same way. Mary Mowbray-Clarke, a New York dealer and early pa-

tron, thought these works were caricatures or burlesques of his previous paintings. But they were, in effect, self-portraits, like the houses. Evidently, Burchfield found them too distasteful and destroyed most of them shortly after.

The dislocations within Burchfield's soul corresponded to larger dislocations of the American spirit after World War I. Although insulated, he was not isolated, and the houses as well as the birds paralleled the intellectual and emotional hesitations then descending on American cultural life.

THE SPECIFIC focus of Burchfield's relationship to the newly emerging cultural patterns altered considerably in 1919, and a divide clearly began to appear, separating his early work from the new direction it had begun to take. For the time being, many of the thoughts and proposals about painting first articulated in 1915 and reduced to a negative distillation in 1919 were shelved, not to be fully revived until the mid-1940s. The spiritual journey Burchfield took

in the intervening years was one shared by many.

The primary vehicles for his newly developing attitude were buildings—residential, industrial, commercial—but not the hallucinated types of 1918, although some of these lingered on for a while. The rundown buildings, more realistically portrayed, that he found in Salem and nearby towns, effectively conveyed his new, less highly charged responses to his subject matter. Where earlier he had found houses moody and humanoid in character, he now became enamored of their picturesqueness and hoped, as he said, that the curse of physical improvement would not be visited upon them.

His concern for their preservation as well as his willingness to reveal their decay reflected similar ambivalent feelings about that old, tired place called "home" that Middle Western writers were beginning to express. Perhaps the catalytic agent for Burchfield was Sherwood Anderson's *Winesburg, Ohio,* a book he read in 1919. At a time when he was floundering, it helped him begin to feel the poetry of the Middle West, often an elegy, and his own life in relation to it. He began to look upon the streets and the buildings of the Middle West, with their timbered false fronts and weathered boards, as aspects of American life rather than as images containing a private content.

Of these buildings he later said, "If I presented them in all their garish and crude primitiveness and unlovely decay, it was *merely* through a desire to be honest about them."[15] His honesty may also have been prompted by another writer Burchfield discovered at this time, the Russian, Maxim Gorky, in whose works he could find many searing images of derelict people and tawdry surroundings. Occasionally, Burchfield chose to indict modern society and, very rarely, he might paint a scene evocative of a work such as *The Lower Depths*. But he usually remained aloof from specific human issues and rarely studied the victims of industrial development directly. Political considerations rarely motivated him.

IT WAS NOT with European but with American writers that Burchfield's paintings bear closest comparison, especially with those who participated in the broad and scattered movement known as the Revolt from the Village. Its chief figures included Sherwood Anderson, Edgar Lee Masters, Sinclair Lewis, and Zona Gale, among others. Their examinations of the Spoon Rivers, Gopher Prairies, and Winesburgs of the Middle West brought to the public's attention, in Lewis Mumford's memorable phrase, " . . . the pathology, not the heroism of the pioneer."[16]

Part of the rediscovery of America that took place during the 1920s, the movement destroyed many myths and shibboleths about the Middle West, particularly the belief that the American small town was a place of innocence and virtue, a paradise compared to the hell of living in the big city. Beginning with Masters' *Spoon River Anthology,* written in 1914–15 and the opening salvo of the Revolt, the havoc a small town could play in the lives of both sensitive

GATES DOWN, *1920, gouache and watercolor, 18 1/16" x 23 15/16". Courtesy Museum of Art, Rhode Island School of Design.*

FACTORY TOWN SCENE, *1920–29, watercolor, 14" x 20". Courtesy Newark Museum.*

and ordinary people was de-
lineated with grisly precision.
The writers of the Revolt placed
little confidence in democracy or
believed it capable of releasing
positive forces of human energy.
Instead, they saw it as a means of
cultivating uniformity rather than
unity in its inhabitants. With
meanness and hypocrisy domi-
nant themes in these novels of
small-town life, the writers described democracy as ensuring
triumphant mediocrity at the ex-
pense of creativity. They described unwholesome reverence
for the blandly average which
dominated life. The pioneering
heritage had long since decayed
and their works mourned whatever was left of the spirit that was
fast exhausting itself.

The writers also carefully observed the repressive tendencies
of Middle Westerners and the
emotional barrenness of their
lives. One passage in *Winesburg,
Ohio* catches well the flavor of
these observations. An alcoholic
says in one of the stories, "Drink
is not the only thing to which I am
addicted. There is something
else. I am a lover and have not
found my thing to love. That is a

big point if you know enough to
realize what I mean."[17]

As the novelists and short-
story writers picked apart the
emptiness of contemporary life,
critics and historians extended
the chronological range of con-
demnation to include the post—
Civil War decades, the 1870s,
1880s, and 1890s. In one of the
greatest debunkings of an era
ever encountered in American
cultural history, that earlier
period was blamed for many contemporary ills.

In those decades of industrial
pioneering, when business absorbed the psychic energies of
the American people, the re-
sources of the continent were or-
ganized and exploited. But the
critics found the costs in im-
poverished spiritual sustenance
and the stunting of esthetic
growth excessive. The roots of the
stifling conventionality of small-
town life were thought to have
been nurtured at that time, as
Van Wyck Brooks said, when in
the horizonless Middle West a
sort of unconscious conspiracy
actuated all America against the
creative life.[18]

Even the literary figures of the

period were criticized severely
and were considered far inferior
to Emerson and Thoreau, their
immediate predecessors. The
spiritual nullity of the period, it
was felt, had crushed their already too-slender talents.

Architecture had as little
chance against the critical on-
slaught as literature. Two sentences in Lewis Mumford's *Sticks
and Stones,* a pioneering history
of American Architecture,
limned the field to be attacked:

> With the little eddies of eclecticism,
> with the rage for the Mansard roof, or
> the introduction of German Gothic,
> and a little later [1880s], the taste
> for Queen Anne domesticity, there
> is scarcely any need to deal: they
> represented only the dispersion of
> taste and the collapse of judgement
> which marked the Gilded Age . . . .
> In the awkward country villas that
> began to fill the still remote suburbs
> of the larger cities, all sense of style
> and proportion were lost: the plan
> was marked by meaningless
> irregularities, a dingy, muddy color
> spread over the wooden facades.[19]

Why the vitriol? Why the great
contempt for the present and for
the earlier years? Both periods
had much in common, and
perhaps the critics used the ear-

lier period as a scapegoat for the evils of their own time, which the novelists were clearly revealing. Both periods followed major wars; into each could be read the frustrations of American society; and each, in the administrations of Grant and Harding, had its appropriate symbol of corruption.

In any event, the debunking mood lasted a decade. By 1930, attitudes toward both periods softened considerably. The achievements of the earlier writers and architects were better understood and the Revolt from the Village turned into a Regionalist attack on the big cities.

Burchfield, the only major painter who can be associated with the critical Middle Western writers, plainly revealed his sympathies with their aims, if with a milder sense of recrimination and outrage. His connection with them was not an intimate one, however. He probably knew none personally, but was familiar with them through their writings. Whether he would have evolved the style and subject matter he employed during the 1920s without knowing their work is, of course, speculative. But so wide-spread did the Revolt from the Village become and so profound were the attacks on the post—Civil War era that it would have been difficult not to be affected even if one made a conscious effort to ignore them.

But the Middle Western subject matter masked an even more profound correspondence of attitude between Burchfield and the writers. Their art was not personal and introspective, but was developed in close touch with public consciousness. Their artistic statements were those which grew from, reflected, interacted with, and were critical of the lives of common people. The idea of a communicating art was more important than individual fulfillment or unique adventure. Content rather than technique was the prime consideration.

AROUND 1920, Burchfield began to explore hamlets and villages to the southeast of Salem, toward the Ohio River. They extended a few streets deep, shoved against the river's edge by the rolling hills just beyond. Many, already withered before their time, had seen their significant growth ended by 1890. Few of the important residences or business and public buildings on their principal streets were erected after that time. Their industrial buildings, physically cramped, mean, and dirty, cast a heavy gloom over the immediate landscape.

When painting these buildings, Burchfield paid careful attention to their nuances of shape and form, clearly distinguishing French mansard houses from Italian villa dwellings. His attention to detail makes the paintings compendiums of the vernacular architectural ornament used in those days. He indulged in a nostalgia for a lost past, hunting after the beauty, real or imagined, that lurked behind a cracked column or a few rows of faded wood siding.

Yet the buildings looked unloved, certainly uncared for. The structural decay of some and the rotted clapboards of others tarnished the elegance they once possessed. Physically bankrupt, they suggested the spiritual prostration of that earlier time. But Burchfield was a romantic poet in the end, and he seemed

17. Bouquet II, *1925, watercolor on paper, 17-1/2″ x 17-1/2″.*
Courtesy Mr. and Mrs. Mortimer Spiller, Buffalo, New York.

18. MARCH WIND, *1926, watercolor on paper, 26-1/2" x 39-3/4". Courtesy The Cleveland Museum of Art, The J. H. Wade Fund.*

19. AUGUST AFTERNOON, *1927, watercolor on paper, 23-3/8" x 32-3/8". Courtesy The Metropolitan Museum of Art, Jessup Fund.*

20. Winter Twilight, *1927–30, oil on composition board, 27-3/4" x 30-1/2". Courtesy The Whitney Museum of American Art.*

21. RAINY NIGHT, *1929–30, watercolor on paper, 30" x 42". Courtesy The Fine Arts Gallery of San Diego, Gift of Misses Anne R. and Amy Putnam.*

22. END OF THE DAY, *1936–38, watercolor on paper, 28" x 48". Courtesy Pennsylvania Academy of the Fine Arts.*

23. BLACK IRON (ERIE AND N.Y. CENTRAL RR BRIDGES OVER BUFFALO RIVER), *1935, watercolor on paper, 29" x 41". Courtesy Private Collection.*

24. THE SKY BEYOND, *1940, watercolor on paper, 20" x 24". Courtesy Addison Gallery of American Art, Phillips Academy, Andover, Mass.*

25. THE EDGE OF TOWN, *1921–41, watercolor on paper, 27" x 40". Courtesy Nelson Gallery–Atkins Museum (Friends of Art Collection).

26. THE COMING OF SPRING, *1917–43, watercolor on paper, 34" x 48". Courtesy The Metropolitan Museum of Art, George A. Hearn Fund.*

27. AUTUMNAL FANTASY, *1917–44, watercolor on paper, 37" x 52-1/2". Courtesy Kennedy Galleries, Inc., New York.*

28. The Sphinx and the Milky Way, *1946, watercolor on paper, 52-5/8" x 44-3/4".*
Courtesy Munson-Williams-Proctor Institute, Edward W. Root Bequest.

29. HUSH BEFORE THE STORM, *1947, watercolor on paper, 22" x 34". Courtesy Wichita Art Museum, Wichita, Kansas.*

30. WINTER SUN AND BARNYARDS, *1947, watercolor on paper, 26" x 34-1/8". Courtesy Dr. and Mrs. Meyer Riwchun, Buffalo, New York.*

31. FLAME OF SPRING, *1948, watercolor on paper, 40" x 30". Courtesy Munson-Williams-Proctor Institute, Edward W. Root Bequest.*

rather to caress the derelict structures than to savage them. He found delight in their frayed textures, their odd shingling, and their multihued stains. As he earlier looked intently at trees, he now contemplated the old buildings and took what visual poetry he could find there.

Burchfield did not merely chronicle the streets of these towns. Although he abandoned the old fantasies after 1920, he still enjoyed painting spiritually unified scenes in which mood, weather, and buildings all evoked similar feelings. In fact, in a number of variations over the years, he could find corresponding weather patterns to match the mood created by a particular industrial or urban scene. With remarkable sensitivity, he achieved a unified focus of feeling in *Factory Town Scene*. He sought that moment at the end of a temporary winter thaw when the soggy and soot-stained air begins to grow cold, sharpening the edges of forms and heralding the approach of a snow storm. At the same time, he wanted to show a town dominated by heavy factory smoke which, hovering like a

pall, holds all things shrouded in terror, as if anticipating the arrival of a calamity. The manmade overcast, then, is equated with one of nature's own devising, and both suggest approaching disaster.

Burchfield's acute awareness of the multiplicity of sensations inherent in the scene provided this somber view with a contrasting richness of feeling. We can respond both rationally and with animal intuition to the impending change. To one who has witnessed the arrival of such a storm, the painting recalls the actual physical, emotional, and visual effects experienced at the time.

The main streets of factory towns or trading centers usually appeared as mutations on the landscape. They consisted of a few large boxes tasseled with a kind of garish ornamentation that made everything else look awkward and cheap. On either side of the central block a few additional houses dribbled off into the countryside. In at least three similar paintings, Burchfield painted for all time the Middle Western main street, circa 1890, which, now trimmed with neon and plastic,

still seems as physically demoralized as ever. We seek in vain for a sign of life in that pastiche of materials and ornament, and search fruitlessly for sustaining roots in the soil.

Burchfield's views of the main drag are the classic painterly equivalents of those more westerly main streets described by Hamlin Garland and Sinclair Lewis (color plates 13, 20, and 25).

The town caught and held his eyes first. How poor and dull and sleepy and squalid it seemed! The one main street ended at the hillside at his left, and stretched away to the north, between two rows of the usual village stores, unrelieved by a tree or a touch of beauty. An unpaved street, with walled, drab-colored, miserable, rotting wooden buildings, with the inevitable battlements: the same—only worse and more squalid—was the town.[20]

Main Street with its two-story brick shops, its story-and-a-half wooden residences, its muddy expanse from concrete walk to walk, its huddle of Fords and lumber-wagons, was too small to absorb her. The broad, straight, unenticing gashes of the streets let in the grasping prairie on every side. She realized the vastness and emptiness of the land. . . .

She thought of the coming of the Northern winter, when the unprotected houses would crouch together in terror of storms galloping out of that wild waste. They were so small and weak, the little brown houses. They were shelters for sparrows, not homes for warm, laughing people.[21]

The repressive qualities Burchfield found in the towns seeped out into the surrounding fields, if in different ways. Here, the contrast between man and the universe, rather than that between man and his community, can be observed. In the roads that traversed the landscape, the fields that were plowed into it, and the houses and barns that were built upon it he tried to suggest the epic grandeur of post-pioneer life, the struggle with the land, and the energies exhausted upon it. Not a mythmaker, Burchfield depicted the results of that meeting between the settler and the land, the beauty inherent in the meeting, and the scars each left on the other.

In the new literature, he could have found ample encouragement for his growing interest in the landscape as the Middle Western landscape. He read the novels of Willa Cather and may

well have found in them images for his mind's eye, perhaps the most essential one being that of the hard-working individual trying to send down roots into the recalcitrant soil.

A particular passage from Zona Gale's *Lulu Bett*, set in the town of Warbleton, a Scylla to Winesburg's Charybdis, prompted the first version of *November Evening*. After Lulu, the introverted older maiden sister and beast of burden of a frighteningly provincial family is introduced, this line appears: "It is said that if our sun were as near to Arcturus as we are near to our sun, the great Arcturus would burn our sun to nothingness."[22]

To Burchfield, this passage engendered a host of reflections concerning the vastness of the Middle Western sky and the way it seemed to overwhelm the habitations and efforts of man. Filtered through the cloth of his imagination, the image of a farmer and his team approaching a desultory crossroads hamlet began to appear under an ample and ultimately opaque sky. Their progress between land and sky assumed the understated central drama of the painting. In the final

version, the houses, once hallucinated in the manner of 1918, have grown firm, as if their roots have finally taken hold in the soil. No glory song, nor yet a facile deprecation of that struggle for settlement which Gale and Cather noted, Burchfield's painting is one of the great statements about the Western settlement.

Another aspect of the Western settlement, which aroused Burchfield's interest rather than passion, was the railroad. Trains, the most visible link with the outside world, signified exhilaration, fantasy, and mystery, as well as enduring strength. His interest in and fascination with them were no different from those of any young boy and man who grew up in a small town around the turn of the century.

Perhaps Sinclair Lewis in *Main Street* best expressed the enchantment trains held for those who heard a steam whistle blow. "The railroad was more than a means of transportation to Gopher Prairie. It was a new god; a monster of steel limbs, oak ribs, flesh, and a stupendous hunger for freight; a deity created by man . . . . "[23]

The rails, to a young boy hop-

Nᴏᴠᴇᴍʙᴇʀ Eᴠᴇɴɪɴɢ, *1939, oil on canvas, 32 1/8" x 52". Courtesy The Metropolitan Museum of Art, George A. Hearn Fund.*

RAILROAD GANTRY, *1920, watercolor, 18" x 24 5/8". Courtesy Museum of Modern Art, New York*.

"...life, with all that the word implies, is of first importance to me."

ping on them, knew no natural boundaries. They terminated only at the ends of the continent. Like the principal character of *Winesburg, Ohio,* who at the book's end leaves town by train, the rails could carry one away to a new life and to adventure.

As a young man, Burchfield felt that the movements of locomotives shifting back and forth were "the powerful, freakish poetry" of his town and that the scream of their whistles jarred the air and called to mind "long, flat romantic stretches of rails."[24]

The mature Burchfield found entire freight yards filled with sensuous pleasures for the eye, ear, and nose. On one visit, he felt that the "... soot and smoke-blacked surfaces, the coal-dust-filmed earth, the gleaming rails, the sturdy, grimy men, even the bitter, acrid odor of the hot, grey-violet smoke was far from disagreeable." For him, even the spaces between freight cars could, as he said, be as important as shades of political complexities.[25]

The lure of the trains even prompted Burchfield to accept one of his very few commissions.

In 1938, he painted the railroad yards at Altoona and Harrisburg, Pennsylvania, for *Fortune* magazine.

A LTHOUGH Burchfield's middle period is largely associated with the painting of buildings, he continued to create a significant number of landscapes, but only by implication did many invoke a specific Middle Western flavor. The landscape he envisioned remained his private preserve. It was no longer populated with the chimeras of the earlier days, but he still used it to reveal a wide range of intense emotions— from gloom and despair to fervent affirmation. In the paintings of one of his favorite themes, the apocalyptic landscape, there were thoroughly blighted versions that looked as if the warming and life-giving rays of the sun would never work their magic and others in which a marvelously ardent and sensuous handling of earth, trees, and clouds turned the countryside into perpetual summer (color plate 16).

He would always respond to the landscape by maintaining a constantly high-pitched sensitiv-

ity to its many nuances. Even in 1929, during a period when the painting of buildings was uppermost in his mind, he often sketched outdoors. On one particular early fall day the weather was so perfect that he felt as if he had just completed his very first walk in the woods: the first man in a new land.

He seemed to feel the physical presence of the woods more easily in the 1920s because it no longer served as a medium for his fantasies of the past. The swamps and paths and clumps of bushes became areas to record sensations rather than arenas to provoke reveries. More realistically painted than before, their spaces became visually measurable, but not physically traversable. That his landscapes would never become, no matte—how realistically he painted them. One could only enter them by an emotional, not a physical, leap.

Although he no longer visualized woodland sounds, he still painted woodland creatures, and he used them as symbols for the seasons of the year. Horses, representing October, might gallop as if their open and free movement cast off the constrictions of

117

September's late-summer heat. Two birds, representing the energies of March, cavort on tree branches, their songs carrying on the procreative warm winds. In paintings such as these, he is still the celebrant of old, using himself as an instrument of nature's changing moods (color plate 18).

As Burchfield's paintings grew increasingly realistic, the stylistic traits used earlier to such good effect were discarded for new ones. He largely abandoned the flat-patterned cutout effects, so that buildings look increasingly less abstract and approximate more nearly their actual appearances. Definitions of objects grew clearer. Windows lost their blind-eyed stares, and the textures of wood sidings conformed increasingly to fact.

His handling of space grew more logical, too. Forms began to recede coherently and assume their rightful size in relation to other forms. Although buildings were usually placed frontally, an increasing number were approached from a diagonal position, thus opening up the possibilities of spatial exploitation (color plate 14). But even in these, Burchfield usually limited the distances. Not a painter of panoramas, he needed the feeling of intimacy with his subjects which he could project only in shallow spaces.

SUGGESTING bulk and weight rather than manipulating surface effects became a central concern. Buildings might not only symbolize the characters of their inhabitants, they could shelter them and resist punishing storms. To complement the increasing realization of the specific gravity of the structures, trees were painted more reasonably, if not always more realistically. Whiplash lines disappeared and with them the linear formulations that carried an arabesque across one object to another.

Burchfield's handling of composition grew noticeably tighter during the 1920s. But his painting never became an intellectual exercise for stating a theory of art or manipulating a sequence of abstract relationships. As extensions of his own feelings, his paintings remained structurally flexible, responding to a whim or a long-felt desire rather than to the exacting needs of compositional balance. To be sure, balance is evident—some busy brushwork on one side of a watercolor that corresponds to a large shape on the other; a horizontal pattern making its way across a variety of forms—but Burchfield's strength, even in his middle phase, lay more in the character he brought to a painting than in its construction. In fact, he is one of the few important painters in whose work perception of the underlying structure is not a basic function of understanding or appreciation.

This is one of Burchfield's great strengths, and it helps explain the way in which simple backyard scenes can transform themselves into profound statements about life in small-town America. Since the forms are not always contained within cohesive frameworks, they are not set off too distinctly from the viewer's own world. Their connection with actual life seems to be imminent and possible, and encourages the viewer to indulge his own memories or speculations about the way people in Burchfield's houses conduct their lives. His paintings, therefore, can become points of departure for an active

SNOW PATTERNS, *1920, watercolor, 14 1/4" x 31". Courtesy Frank Rehn Gallery, New York.*

interior monolog in the viewer's mind. Art does not necessarily get in the way of life. In that delicate balance between recording objects and feelings on the one hand, and creating patterns and managing colors on the other, the scales were tipped in the direction of the former. In this regard, Burchfield's observation in regard to Edward Hopper's painting might just have easily been made about his own: "This sense of a brooding moment in the life of a human being is encountered again and again."[26]

What of purely esthetic criteria? This question, often raised in the 1920s and 1930s, invariably involved comparisons with modern European painting. Some painters, challenged at the most fundamental level of their artistic beings, simply tried to shout down European achievements. They demonstrated their competance and relevance by denigrating the modernists.

Others adopted a position not unlike John Marin's. He criticized Cézanne because the Frenchman was concerned only with art, not with both art and life. Burchfield's position was similar. When he finally learned about modern Parisian modes, he did not become antagonistic, but he did not have many kind words either. He was not a polemicist, pitting American against European art or native tradition against imported innovation. Rather, modernist painting did not suit his aims in art. He made no excuses or untenable assertions. "Stating it as simply as I can," he once said, "I am one who finds himself in an incredibly interesting world, and my chief concern is to record as many of my impressions as possible, in the simplest and most forthright manner. In short, life, with all that the word implies, is of first importance to me."[27] By comparison, he found abstract art a worthwhile refuge for those who wanted to avoid all unpleasant contact with the world.

The operative word for Burchfield was "life." He could have used "reality," but that might have implied philosophical postulates concerning its nature, and these might have encased his art within a theory. He obviously preferred to respond to what his senses told him. His distrust of intellectual assumptions was a typically American trait, and if that meant ignoring modernist art, it was a decision easily reached.

OLD FARM HOUSE (SEPTEMBER SUNLIGHT), *1932, watercolor, 14 7/8" x 21".*
Courtesy Fogg Art Museum, Harvard University, Louise E. Bettens Fund.

PAINTING
THE AMERICAN
SCENE

Old Tavern at Hammondsville, Ohio, *1926–28, watercolor, 25 3/4" x 33". Courtesy Addison Gallery of American Art, Phillips Academy.*

. . . the old swimming hole, the shack in the woods, and the Fourth of July oration . . .

ALTHOUGH Burchfield exhibited in New York City as early as 1916 and again in 1920, he did not begin to receive significant notice until the mid-twenties. Implicit in his critical recognition was his identification with the Revolt from the Village, at first vaguely patronizing, but then more accepting as critics began actively searching for a modern, but not modernist, American art.

He became known, through his bleak townscapes, as the artist best able to represent the inwardness of the Middle Western small town. He was called the Sinclair Lewis of the paintbrush, the artist who most cogently dramatized the world of contemporary American civilization.

The range of compliments was quite broad, but in the parlance of the late 1920s and early 1930s, it conveyed specific meanings. By the end of the 1920s, many artists had begun to paint the countryside and its small towns in both appreciative and joyless manners. They became known as American Scene painters or Regionalists. As a movement, regionalism developed without specific style or program, or even an artistic center. But central to its progress was the desire to forge an American art from American materials. Generally anti-European and anti-modernist in sentiment, it considered abstract art an exhausted congeries of styles already a generation or two past its prime. Implicit in its rejection of European modernism was an acceptance of homespun, traditional values, an easy communicability of subject matter, and a willingness of artists to become active, responsive members of society. What had been considered negative traits in the American character in 1920 now assumed new virtue. Those earlier considered positive were now amplified.

To chauvinist critics like Thomas Craven, the American artist was duty bound to forsake radical experiments and to Paint American. Only then, would American art free itself from its position as a colonial outpost of European art and reflect instead the emerging American civilization. The hinterlands, satirized in the early 1920s, now became the repository of whatever intellectual and moral strength the country possessed. To a variety of critics, art dealers, and museum curators, including those in New York City, the new painting of America was emerging in the Middle West.

These considerations reflected a broad spectrum of attitudes at both the highest academic levels and in the meanest backwoods' clubhouses. The theories of the historian Frederick Jackson Turner concerning the impact of the frontier on American democracy achieved their greatest popularity in the 1920s. By 1930, regional research in the social sciences and a creative regional literature flourished, especially in the south, both on and off college campuses.

At the same time, a virulent strain of nativism, nourished by fears of urbanization, the dilution of the old Anglo-Saxon stock, and the submerging of old, trusted values by new, alien ones, dominated the minds of many inhabitants of Middle America. Hankering after an earlier, noninternationalized, nonurban, nonmechanized America, those persons who espoused nationalism and regionalism at whatever level of sophistication were afraid of losing what was already slipping away. In McLuhanesque terms, the old, rural, small-town environment, or the past, became the content of an art produced in an increasingly industrial environment.

BURCHFIELD, who had been painting the American scene before those words identified the movement, was given greatest credit for turning the attention of painter and public alike to the old native environment. It no longer mattered that his views had once been considered critical. After the rapid industrialization and urbanization that occurred in the 1920s, and the mergence of a technocratic society, his work formed a ready source of imagery for that marvelous and probably imaginary place called home: ramshackle yet solid, simple and unpretentious. The paintings suggested the kind of roots many yearned for. Perhaps the very grimness of his scenes contributed to their great popularity, calling Americans back from the long holiday of the boom period to the more sober-sided life that was

their true inheritance. The paintings, then, were a conscience and a guide; a reminder of what were truly American experiences.

Characteristically, Burchfield remained aloof from the organizational aspects of the American Scene movement and even denied that he was ever a part of it. His old teacher, Henry Keller, had believed, prophetically, that the significant American culture of the future would spring from the Middle West and that the old swimming hole, the shack in the woods, and the Fourth of July oration would be important parts of that culture. Burchfield ignored the vogue and insisted that he painted for no particular audience, but for anybody, anywhere, who felt spiritual kinship with his works.

At a time when other artists were scrambling for a place on the bandwagon, he found American Scene painting as significant as any other type, but no more so. His own personal responses to a scene were motivation enough to put brush to paper. "While I feel strongly the personality of a given scene, its genius loci, as it were,"

he once said, "my chief aim in painting is the expression of a completely personal mood."[28]

Nevertheless, his personal moods coincided with those of many other artists, and his protestations may have been motivated in part by his need for isolation. Certainly his paintings of streets, houses, and the countryside provided numerous clues for younger painters; his work was among the most imitated of any artist's during the 1930s.

When he did think of painting something typically American—it was impossible not to escape such thoughts during that decade—he did so on levels far more complex than simply chronicling regional histories, topical events, or topographical features. He wanted somehow to embrace the epic poetry that America represented. In 1932, while musing about Sibelius' *Finlandia,* a work he felt captured the spirit of an entire nation, the desire grew in him to create a painting that would do the same for America.

Clearly, his secluded life in a suburb of Buffalo and his disinterest in painting mural cycles, then just becoming popular, re-

EVENING, *1932, watercolor, 31 1/2" x 43 1/2". Courtesy Newark Museum.*

FREIGHT CARS UNDER A BRIDGE, *1933, watercolor, 24" x 34". Courtesy The Detroit Institute of Arts, Gift of Dr. and Mrs. George Kamperman.*

THE PARADE, *1934, watercolor, 25" x 37". Courtesy Dr. and Mrs. Irving Frederick Burton.*

stricted his possibilities. But in a number of paintings done soon after he did allude to aspects of the American spirit and, at the same time, captured better than any of his contemporaries the qualities of small-town and rural American life in that difficult decade.

IN THE FULL maturity of his middle years, he was able to call on an extensive technique and a practical familiarity with his subject matter, and for the first time in his career, he was able to create works in which his own presence was not so keenly marked. Perhaps the Depression joggled his mind, causing him to respond more to impulses given off by his subjects rather than to mirror his own feelings in them. In any event, works like *Evening, November Evening, The Parade, Freight Cars Under a Bridge, End of the Day* (color plate 22), and *Black Iron* (color plate 23) are among his great "public" paintings. Looking at them, one worries less about the state of Burchfield's mind and feelings than the flood of meanings the paintings suggest. They

are not as autobiographical as the earlier pieces, or at least the autobiographical elements seem less important.

Still, Burchfield's own imaginings never lurked too far beneath the surface. In the hands of a local colorist, *Evening* could have become a showcase of upper-Appalachian eccentricities. Instead, Burchfield preferred to use the lush setting to describe the evening of a day, the evening of a year when nature has spent itself, the evening of the peoples' lives, the evening of a phase of American farm life. Although ostensibly about American farmers, the painting is also about the interacting nuances of age, weather, and nature.

Burchfield said that *The Parade* was the only Depression picture he ever painted.
In that he depicted militant workers on strike, it is, for he never explored this or related themes again nor did he examine in a documentary way human suffering during those hard times.

The painting developed from an experience shared with his wife one day in Buffalo when a parade of unemployed workers

blocked their way. He felt that if nothing were done to alleviate conditions, society would soon crumble. This feeling was translated into pictorial terms by showing the strikers through openings in a cracked, concrete bridge. The bridge itself provides an appropriate tomblike quality, and the cracks symbolize the stresses to society's foundations.

As the Depression deepened and the economy stagnated, Burchfield's subject matter also seemed to slow down, especially the railroad scenes. Once showing great activity, they now lost their pulsating life force. Freight cars stood idle and engines were quiet. Even great machines seemed poised, ready to function, but remaining immobile (color plate 21). Never before in his work, nor later, would so many large mechanical forms seem so inert and so incapable of motion. These paintings seem perfect visual metaphors for the industrial statistics then being issued by the government; in their way, they effectively capture the depressed spirit of the economy and of the country as a whole.

Buildings that ran down curv-

THE HAY MOW (SUGAR TREE
ALLEY, SALEM, OHIO), *1924,
wood engraving cut by Julius
A. Lankes, #17 of an edition of
25, 178 x 255mm. This is one
of a series of wood engravings
that were cut by Lankes from
drawings by Burchfield between
1923–26. Courtesy Mr. and
Mrs. Mortimer Spiller.*

THE HAYMOW, *1920, watercolor, 20 3/4" x 29 1/2". Courtesy Mr. Edward D. Whelan, Sr.*

THE FALSE FRONT, *1920–21, watercolor, 21" x 30". Courtesy The Metropolitan Museum of Art, New York, Rogers Fund.*

CIVIC IMPROVEMENT, *1927–28, watercolor, 27″ x 36″. Courtesy Collection IBM Corporation.*

LILACS, *1924–27, oil, 23 1/2" x 35". Courtesy Delaware Art Museum*.

**If these scenes speak
of a great sorrow on the land,
they also allude to the resilience
of the people who lived on it.**

MARCH, *1923–28, tempera 29 1/4" x 42". Courtesy Delaware Art Museum.*

THE OPEN ROAD, *1931, watercolor, 24 1/4" x 33 1/4". Courtesy Katrina McCormick Barnes.*

ing Ohio streets sagged more appreciably than they did in the 1920s, as if on each return visit Burchfield wanted to record their aging (color plate 22). Where earlier they had only seemed gaunt, they now appeared haggard, like their inhabitants. Such works recall his admonition of the early 1920s to indict fearlessly the failures of modern society, but these are not political paintings as the phrase was then understood. They did not advance a political cause or philosophy and they were not painted in partisan anger. Nor were they a call to arms: Burchfield was not a creator of propaganda.

If these scenes speak of a great sorrow on the land, they also allude to the resilience of the people who lived on it. Burchfield painted the old, weatherbeaten houses as if they had grown from the earth. They seem symbolic of the indestructibility of man, a revelation of his dignity. Despite adversity, both houses and men were surviving, and in a way unknown to those who had never suffered.

Far removed from the debunking spirit of the 1920s, *End of the Day* commands a reluctant admiration for the town, its inhabitants, and their gritty determination to persevere. Because of the way in which it lays bare the lives of the industrial workers, it is an effective pendant to the final version of *November Evening* (see page 114. In that work, Burchfield wanted to express the hardships of rural life in the Middle West. Together, these two works, really great tragic-triumphant paintings of the settlement of the land, may come closest to what he had in mind when reflecting upon *Finlandia*.

THE BLACK BARN, *1930, watercolor 23" x 31 1/2". Courtesy Indianapolis Museum of Art, Marla Delzell Memorial Fund.*

ABANDONED FARMHOUSE, *1932, watercolor, 23 1/2" x 33". Courtesy The University of Nebraska Art Galleries, F . M . Hall Collection.*

MOVE TOWARD REALISM

THE OPEN DOOR, *1932, watercolor, 27" x 36". Courtesy Kennedy Galleries, New York.*

. . . he became obsessed with the idea that he had lost his sense of direction.

AS IF TO emphasize the gravity of the period as well as of his subject matter, Burchfield's technique grew increasingly subdued. Striking contrasts of color and value diminished, so that a greater evenness of effect came to characterize the works of the 1930s. More often than not, skies became more palpable, with richer textures substituting for the earlier neutral backgrounds. With more careful attention to modeling and to natural lighting effects, these works possess a unique density. Forms sit firmly on the ground. Windowframes open upon interior rooms rather than act as borders of flattened patterns.

The earlier fantasy and casual dexterity give way to a sobriety even more measured than in the 1920s. If Burchfield's art gained in structural richness and narrative profundity, it lost some of its visionary inventiveness and fanciful insubstantiality. His art was moving toward the interest in realistic painting then reigning in the country. As his art grew less immediately personal, it increasingly reflected acknowledgment of the public's desire for recognizable, easily identifiable imagery and shared experiences.

If there is a year that may be called Burchfield's most realistic, it was 1932–33. It may be measured by his studies of lighting conditions. Only at that time did he study them so acutely or record their effects so consistently across a painting's surface. In pictures of farmhouses and ships, he used light to define the three-dimensionality of forms and he let it subtly establish the spaces containing them. Since he had been painting realistic views for more than ten years, the wonder is not that he finally became concerned with precise atmospheric effects but that he waited so long to do so. Interestingly, this most realistic phase occurs virtually in the middle of his second period. It marks, as it were, the apogee of his realism, and in another ten years he would once again begin to explore the visions and fantasies of his youth.

Although Burchfield painted with seemingly little effort during the 1930s, he often fretted over his work. Repeatedly, he felt that he was growing stale and spending too much time in his studio, rather than being outdoors. He always felt the need to paint in front of his subjects, to feel and to experience those emotional states brought about by the actual presence of the landscape.

In 1935, he momentarily revived a mode he had used in the 1920s. Worried that this throwback might indicate a weakening or a low period, he nevertheless enjoyed the uncalculated nature of this experiment. It was as if he often argued with himself as he weighed the value of each stroke, painting quite self-consciously, but preferring not to think so carefully about what he was doing. At a time when his art was most calculated, he longed for directness of response and immediacy of feeling.

He still hiked and sketched in the woods near his home, and his paintings of landscape scenes probably provided him with the kind of emotional release he needed. Although these nature paintings were more realistic than the earlier ones, they made contact with living things and nature's rhythms in a way that houses never could. He still listened to the cadences of crickets, and in the movement of a leaf he could still hear a song. Individual trees, jet black against a sunlit sky or pale on an overcast day, still moved him profoundly. In spring, he enjoyed swampy areas where, around rotted trees, spring peepers and insect larvae sound the new season.

IN RURAL scenes he would reach back to earlier moods and try to summarize a variety of feelings as well as time sequences. If the works reflect a Middle Western flavor, it grew innately from the subjects and their locales rather than from external application of regionalist notions.

In *Lace Gables*, for example, Burchfield evoked a host of impressions. On a summer day, with the air hot and heavy, an ancient house seems to support and be supported by trees and bushes, its once magnificent flanks now half-hidden by the lush greenery. Dark pockets within the foliage suggest cool hideaway places almost as mysterious as the imagined contents of the old, still, and perhaps empty structure. The silences surrounding the house, about to

be broken by an approaching storm, are nevertheless profound, not simply because summer silences lie heavy on the lonely house, but because there is so much to think about, so many thoughts impending. Tuned to the infinite activities and moods of nature, Burchfield found incredible diversity of feeling at the end of that driveway.

This was his milieu, and one wonders why he visited it only occasionally during those years. In 1942, he said that being known as a painter of tired streets annoyed him, especially since he found so many moods worth exploring in nature. He was surprised by his willingness to paint anything else. But obviously he also longed to explore human scenes and could not give these up, either.

Caught between these two apparently contradictory desires, he felt increasingly uneasy about his art. During one bleak moment in 1938, he wrote in his journal that he longed to work in the spontaneous and free manner of 1917. A year later, he said that he felt imprisoned by the old papers, but evidently he was not yet ready to forfeit his realistic

manner for their transparent fantasy. Nevertheless, he suffered an acute attack of nostalgia for the years of his childhood. Clearly, he had begun to feel trapped by his current manner and he became obsessed with the idea that he had lost his sense of direction.

While he felt his art was reaching an impasse, Burchfield, perhaps unknowingly, began to prepare for the sudden shift in attitude which occurred in 1943. At the end of the 1930s and in the first years of the next decade, certain elements once again assumed importance in some, but not all, of his works, and some new features appeared that would be more fully exploited later.

Fluttery and whiplash lines returned as he gave freer rein to the physical act of recording brushstrokes. In their width and individuality of gesture, the strokes reflected his immediate and unpremeditated responses to his subjects. Textures grew looser, and instead of frontal views he once again found an interest in the patterns caused by abrupt perspectival breaks. He painted scenes from a second-story window again, not quite the bedroom

LACE GABLES, *1935, watercolor, 24" x 36". Courtesy Munson-Williams-Proctor Institute, Edward W. Root Bequest.*

THREE BOATS IN WINTER, *1933, watercolor 23 1/8" x 33 1/4".*
Courtesy Museum of Art, Rhode Island School of Design.

BRIDGE IN RAIN, *1938, watercolor, 24" x 29 1/2". Courtesy W. E. Leistner.*

SIX O'CLOCK, *1936, watercolor, 24″ x 30″. Courtesy Everson Museum of Art, Syracuse.*

ROAD IN EARLY SPRING, *1938, watercolor mounted on artist's board, 23" x 28". Courtesy Indianapolis Museum of Art, Gift of Friends of American Art and Friends of Art.*

32. SUN AND ROCKS, *1918–50, watercolor on paper, 40" x 56". Courtesy Albright-Knox Art Gallery, Buffalo, New York, Contemporary Art Fund.*

33. EARLY SPRING SUNLIGHT, *1950, watercolor on paper, 25-1/2" x 31-1/8". Courtesy Dr. and Mrs. Meyer Riwchun, Buffalo, New York.*

34. SONG OF THE TELEGRAPH, *1917–52, watercolor on paper, 34" x 53". Courtesy Mr. and Mrs. John Marin, New York City.*

35. Oncoming Spring, *1954, watercolor on paper, 30" x 40". Courtesy Mrs. Harold L. Olmsted, Springville, New York.*

36. LOCUST TREES IN SPRING, *1955, watercolor, 39-1/2" x 29-1/2".*
Courtesy Mr. and Mrs. Mortimer Spiller, Buffalo, New York.

37. SONG OF THE RED BIRD, *1917–60, watercolor on paper, 35-1/4" x 49-1/2". Courtesy Kennedy Galleries, New York.*

38. SNOWFLAKES IN OCTOBER, *1959, watercolor on paper, 44" x 32".*
Courtesy Museum of Fine Arts, Boston, Mass., Charles Henry Hayden Fund.

39. Decement Storm, *1941–60, oil on canvas, 39-3/4" x 55-1/2". Courtesy Charles Burchfield Center,*
State University College at Buffalo, Gift of Mr. and Mrs. Peter C. Andrews.

40. THE FOUR SEASONS, *1949–60, watercolor on pieced sections of paper, mounted on board glazed with plastic, 55-7/8" x 47-7/8".*
Courtesy Krannert Art Museum, University of Illinois, Champaign.

41. CONSTANT LEAF, *1960, watercolor on paper, 39-1/4" x 29-1/4".*
Courtesy Dr. Edna M. Lindemann, Buffalo, New York.

42. Orion in Winter, *1962, oil on canvas, 48" x 54". Courtesy Burchfield Estate.*

43. NORTH WOODS IN SPRING, *1951–64, watercolor on paper, 56" x 40". Courtesy Mr. and Mrs. Keith Davis, Flint, Mich.*

44. DANDELION SEED HEADS AND THE MOON, *1961–65, watercolor on paper, 54-1/4" x 38-1/2".*
Courtesy Kennedy Galleries, New York.

45. SUMMER SOLSTICE, *1961–66, watercolor on paper, 19-1/4" x 27". Courtesy Kennedy Galleries, New York.*

46. HEMLOCK IN NOVEMBER, *1947–66, watercolor on paper, 42-1/2" x 33-1/2". Courtesy Kennedy Galleries, New York.*

DANDELIONS, *1941, watercolor, 24 1/4" x 19 1/2". Courtesy the Burchfield Family.*

OLD HOUSE AND ELM TREES, *1933–40, watercolor, 27" x 40". Courtesy Virginia Museum of Fine Arts.*

SNOWBANK AND POOL, *1936, watercolor, 15" x 24". Courtesy Private Collection.*

of earlier romance, but one which now saw across the tops of nearby buildings or along the edges of his house to yards filled with blooming trees.

Although such scenes were still essentially realistic, their major sections—buildings, fields, skies—arranged themselves into increasingly abstract relationships. Instead of looking at the fundamental three-dimensionality of houses and trees, he began once again, to observe the designs that branches made against a roof or the way in which a building's eavesline turned the sky into a free-form composition.

Houses under sunshine no longer told volumes about an oppressed community, but simply existed on the land. An overcast day was caused by weather conditions, not by sympathy for scarred lives. And single trees, sometimes great, broad ones, filled a painting with feelings of joy and serenity. Less and less an adversary, the earth began to yield up its pleasures once again. It grew increasingly more amiable, offering the kind of place one might want to lie down in and fantasize happily.

FANTASY returned, too, if in small, measured amounts In the last of the "main street" paintings, *Edge of Town* (color plate 25), the mood is considerably less overbearing than earlier (color plate 20). The buildings evoke a greater atmosphere of mystery because of the way light now plays on them, and the sky seems more like a living organism because the open area at the horizon hints at the possibility of sudden atmospheric change.

Although the works of these years might have troubled Burchfield, seen from a later perspective they seem to be among his richest, combining both psychological and stylistic elements from all his previous manners. If they represented to him a pause, it was that kind which suggests a summing up before the start of a new adventure, a gathering of emotional and technical strengths before a new plunge. It was as if he were taking inventory.

The question remained, however: in which direction would he move? Would he explore further eclectic combinations while celebrating the countryside and

its bounty? This might well have suggested to him a kind of retirement, an inability or lack of desire to find stimulation any longer in momentary encounters with nature. As in the year 1918, Burchfield was not willing to settle into the comfortable groove of painting by rote.

Very likely, the effect of World War II contributed to his dissatisfaction. In 1940, he had concluded that an artist should remain aloof from painting war scenes of any sort. Shortly after Pearl Harbor, he ruled out "songs of hate and pessimism" for the duration, a gesture which only made clear in his mind a direction he was already taking. He was left, then, with as William Dean Howells might have said, the more smiling aspects of American scenery.

But like many other artists in a period of ever-widening international strife, Burchfield found the American scene—in any of its aspects—no longer an appropriate source of imagery. Its parachialism seemed harly relevant, its aims grossly inadequate to the global responsibilities being assumed by the nation.

ARTIC OWL AND WINTER MOON, *1960, watercolor, 39″ x 32 1/4″. Courtesy the Burchfield Family.*

THE THIRD PHASE
1943

1967

RETURN
TO
FANTASY

COBWEB HOUSE, *1954, watercolor, 14" x 18". Courtesy Charles H. Renthal.*

. . . butterflies and other insects in constant motion, intoxicated "by the sheer ecstacy of existence."

UNLIKE many other artists, Burchfield had the rich alternative of his imagination to cushion the loss of a viable subject matter. In 1943, he returned to the world of fantasy once again and began to rummage through nature's moods and seasonal variations as well as to hear the sounds of insects and wildflowers growing. The style he developed did not so much reflect the combination of his first and second periods as it revived his early phase, particularly the works of 1917, modified by the later manner.

The change, when it did come, was sudden and well-nigh complete. Within a year, in 1944, he would talk of the preceding twenty-three or twenty-four years of his career as a thing apart from his present work. In renegotiating the terrain of his youth after such a lengthy digression, as he called it, he felt as one reborn. The world was new to him again.

As if to honor his new-found youthful spirit, for the remaining twenty-four years of his life he painted some of the finest celebrations of landscape moods ever done by an American artist. They depended on no particular tradition or style, old or new, and they neither reflected nor activated any mythic images of American art or life. They marked, instead, one of the unique adventures in American art by an artist who, in burrowing deeper into his own soul, brought forth images that repeatedly strike chords of common recognition. He became a fantasist for the public, creating entirely personal pictures, but ones readily understandable and identifiable.

Burchfield used the most direct method possible to revive the fantasies of his youth. He began to complete old studies or to elaborate those already finished by literally adding sections of watercolor paper to them. When possible, he left the early paintings untouched, adding new elements around their peripheries in a similar style. In this way, the old style actually became part of the new, serving as an ever-present source of inspiration and remembrance of the dreams, sounds, and smells he had once visualized and was trying to visualize again.

Working over the old papers must have been a great source of joy to Burchfield. He reveled in closely detailed studies, and he proliferated through his paintings minute observations of plant and insect life. It was his way of entering into those special and private relationships with particular trees or certain bends in the road, or with a familiar clump of Queen Anne's lace, that any woodland wanderer feels. It was also a way of discovering the universe revealed in the pattern the sky makes as it is seen through some leaves or through the darkened boughs of a tree on a winter's day.

The Coming of Spring (color plate 26) was the first painting Burchfield reworked, and it serves as an excellent example of the way his art continually looked back upon itself. It had been left incomplete in 1917. In 1919, he went over it, but removed the added material in 1931. In 1943, he decided to finish the version of 1917 after working on a watercolor begun in 1933 which was itself based on the painting as it existed between 1919 and 1931. The finished work, therefore, received major attention in 1917, 1919, 1931, and 1943, and had at least one satellite, begun in 1933 and based in its appearance on the version that existed between 1919 and 1931.

WHAT WAS originally a fairyland waterfall, and then probably a dispirited gully, reappeared once again as a make-believe hillside with a series of waterfalls. One set, to the left, is already in spring bloom: the other, to the right, is just emerging from winter's darkness. Details are exaggerated: brightly painted lines and strokes, suggesting new blooms, abound. Shadows, appearing virtually as independent darkened lines, barely provide the tree trunks with a three-dimensional feeling. The central, rising hill is brought forward because the intensity of its colors remains stable and does not drift off into an atmospheric purple. As a result, the many forms in the painting exist in an unrealistic, shallow space.

Compared with *The Great Elm* (above), completed only two years before, the spirit and execution of *The Coming of Spring* are quite different. The earlier work records a specific time and place, the later one is located in Burchfield's mind. Although both are landscapes, they clearly show the distance Burchfield traveled in those two years and why he felt the change between the second and third phases was such a profound one.

The first elaborations of the early papers created a problem of scale. The youthful works were usually small in size, and when he enlarged them Burchfield added detail of the same size. On a small sheet, the scale of the detail proved adequate for the overall dimensions, but with additional sheets, the scale became too small. As the details multiplied, paintings ran the risk of appearing too busy and too confusing.

The inadequacy of scale led directly to another problem: the sheer physical presence of so much detail might possibly hinder the evanescent suggestions of fantasy, precisely the quality Burchfield wanted to achieve.

He selected two ways to handle this problem. First, he turned once again to the use of conventions to express moods, but this time he purposely blurred their precise forms and meanings. When loops, spirals, and saddlebacks now appeared, they signified the presence of the artist rather than a specific code by which to read the paintings.

The second way Burchfield ensured the dominance of fantasy over detail was to develop further the brushy techniques that had begun to reappear in the late 1930s. Myriad small strokes, although visible, did not always identify particular objects, but only partially revealed them. Equally important, they gave, in more purely pictorial form, an overall pulsating quality to the paintings. With pigment and brushstroke rather than with identifying detail, Burchfield sought the forces of nature as they coursed through all things. With few distractions, he let the sky, the plants, and the earth throb with equal intensity (color plate 28).

Using this technique, Burchfield painted atmosphere as if it had physical density. Depending on tones and colors, he could suggest the look and feeling of a hot, humid day or the frenzied moments of a snowstorm. He could also keep butterflies and other insects in constant motion, as if they were intoxicated, he once said, "by the sheer ecstacy of existence."[30]

AUGUST MORNING, *1951–59, watercolor, 30" x 40". Courtesy George F. Goodyear.*

SUNSHINE AND RAIN, *1946–47,*
watercolor, 43" x 38".
Courtesy Mrs. Allen Manus.

NIGHT OF THE EQUINOX, *1917–55, watercolor, 40" x 52". Courtesy Sara Roby Foundation.*

CICADA SONG IN SEPTEMBER, *1956, watercolor, 39" x 32 1/2". Courtesy Dr. and Mrs. Theodor Braasch.*

One sees trees, insects, and birds; feels the wind; and hears the forest sounds.

But even if Burchfield wanted to add considerable detail, he was able to manipulate it to good effect, for it did not necessarily have to describe objects entirely of this world. It might also record a series of multi-experiences. Soon after the change of 1943, he began to double and triple the activities occuring within a given area of a painting. Not content with indicating a tree or the sound of insects with short calligraphic strokes, he might superimpose a moth's movements on some leaves, or intermingle clouds with a bush, or soften the edges of trees to suggest the movements of insects (color plate 28).

Such exploitation of detail prevented his paintings from lapsing into static compositions, but instead allowed them to expand in continuous movement. The vital forces of nature surged through his forms, sometimes with seemingly reckless abandon, as if growth and movement were parts of their beings.

ALTHOUGH these paintings are obviously derived from nature, they strike a particularly contemporary note. By intensifying the activities of nature and by showing a variety of them at the same moment, Burchfield suggested a type of time sequence usually associated with modern European and New York–school paintings. It may be called "cinematic time."

In Cubism, for example, a form is observed from different points over a period of time and then reassembled in a series of planes on the picture surface. Or, as in Jackson Pollock's drip paintings, the artist works at them over and over again from four different sides. In both cases, the result is a record of a time flow as if the events had happened in a single instant. Simultaneously, time appears to be stretched out and intensified as one observes the various activities represented.

Burchfield provides a naturalists's version of cinematic time. Instead of a few objects viewed from different perspectives at different times and then superimposed, he brings together a variety of objects and intimations of sounds seen and heard at one moment as well as over a period of time and then superimposes them on the picture surface. One sees trees, insects, and birds; feels the wind; and hears the forest sounds. Each of these elements is isolated, experienced for a few moments, and then mixed with the other elements. The time sequences for each are then stretched out and simultaneously intensified and presented as if they all occurred as Burchfield was able to respond to them at a single instant.

The basis for this extraordinary manipulation of time, very likely unique in modern Western art, lies clearly in observation rather than in theory. Precisely for this reason, these paintings, and similar ones of the 1950s and 1960s, reveal to a remarkable degree the synthesis of traditional American concerns with realism and the landscape with one of the major aspects of modern art.

Indeed, as one looks over the great flowering of Burchfield's art after 1943, comparisons with contemporary idioms, particularly Abstract Expressionism, become inevitable —not to provide him with a backdoor relevancy, but to test his worth against the most vital art movement coincident with his later years.

THE GLORY OF SPRING, *1934–55,*
watercolor, 43" x 54".
Courtesy Mr. and Mrs. Elam Miller.

SUNLIGHT BEHIND TWO PINES, *1957, watercolor, 34" x 48". Courtesy Mr. and Mrs. Malcolm C. Chace, Jr.*

IN THE DEEP WOODS, *1918–56, watercolor, 33" x 45". Courtesy Kennedy Galleries, New York.*

Certainly, many of his paintings show surfaces of remarkable activity and fanciful improvization. Certainly, there are passages of lyrical intensity, spontaneous directness, and profound personal engagement. Burchfield, no less than his younger contemporaries, made that long journey of self-discovery to the center of their own beings, using their art as a naked intermediary between themselves and the world.

But Burchfield's voyage was not based nearly as much on his mind interacting with itself as on a transcendental faith in the operations of nature. To become one with himself, he did not provoke dialog with his unconscious as much as try to let the spirit and moods of nature pass through him. Instead of existential anguish, which takes place in one's mind, Burchfield flung his body on the ground, literally, the better to feel nature's pulse. It was not set-understanding Burchfield was after, but a sense of participation in and reception to the forces that generate from the earth and the heavens.

When Burchfield wrote "The artist must come to nature not with a readymade formula, but in humble reverence, to learn" and "The work of an artist is superior to the surface appearance of nature, but not its basic laws," he was talking about more than finding a sense of structure in nature. He was expressing the conviction that this structure could be recognized in nature's essential life-giving forces. [31]

Of these late works, which share some stylistic features with Abstract Expressionism but are derived from antithetical premises, one is tempted to say that Burchfield took realistic American painting as far as it could go without overtly adopting modern European attitudes, devices, or motivations.

RHAPSODIC
NATURE

PINK LOCUSTS AND WINDY MOON, *1959, watercolor, 32″ x 39″. Courtesy The Chase Manhattan Bank.*

"...something dark and mysterious like a solemn Bach fugue..."

ALTHOUGH he began many new works after 1943, Burchfield often completed older ones. It was his task, he felt, to re-create and reexperience the earlier rhapsodic impressions of life and nature, and he believed that he could successfully reenter that world. As in *The Coming of Spring* (color plate 26) or *Autumnal Fantasy* (color plate 27), he painted in a technique approximating the earlier manner, so that the works appeared unified. In others, however, he juxtaposed different modes. A haunted house of 1919 might appear surrounded by lush vegetation applied with the pulsating strokes typical of the 1940s, or a cluster of flattened, sharp-edged clouds might force itself like an apparition through a brushy assortment of leaves.

Burchfield obviously saw these disparities, but let them remain, perhaps because he did not want to obliterate the memory of the original impulse or perhaps because he wanted to join, but not fuse, the old impulse with the new. The idea of engaging the old with the new, a kind of readymade archaizing, might have prompted him to paint entirely new works which included old-style motifs. In *Pink Locusts and Windy Moon*, for example, the pattern of clouds around the moon and the shadows around the house's windows are reminiscent of early works, yet the painting was begun and completed in 1959.

However Burchfield might manipulate his previous paintings as source material for new ones, it was still his walks in the woods that provided fresh insights. Often, he would write a word picture of a scene to set an appropriate mood before starting to sketch. Sometimes the mood would originate in response to the weather conditions, and sometimes he was already disposed toward a certain feeling and sought a landscape setting equivalent to it. One suspects that more often than not a sketch was the product of the two motives interacting with each other.

Burchfield wrote in his journal the day he began *Hush Before the Storm* (color plate 29) that he wanted to do "... something dark and mysterious like a solemn Bach fugue — something to do with the dark interior of a tree on a cloudy day." In his subsequent word picture of the painting's mood, he described the scene as mid-afternoon in early July. A sudden thunderstorm is rising, but the wind has not yet begun. It is still quiet, but the quiet is ominous. "Deep mystery lurks in the black interior of the trees and the feeling of foreboding is emphasized by the startled white daisies in the foreground."[32]

PRECISELY which came first, the personal mood or the response to approaching bad weather, is, of course, impossible and unnecessary to determine. Of greater importance is Burchfield's desire to evoke rather than to describe. Correspondingly, titles become evocative rather than descriptive. What might have been called *Spring Morning* in 1938 becomes *Flame of Spring* in 1948 (color plate 31). And what might have been a study of a specific locale on an agreeable May morning becomes instead an elicitation of the spirit of spring.

The Coming of Spring, the first work in the new manner, also marked a revival of Burchfield's

EVENING PEACE, *1951, watercolor, 33" x 23". Courtesy Joseph H. Hirshhorn Collection.*

WEATHER MOON, *1960, watercolor, 40" x 29 1/2". Courtesy Dr. and Mrs. Milton Ratner.*

interest in the "all-day" studies he had attempted in 1915. These had originally been inspired by an exhibition of Chinese scroll paintings seen in Cleveland during his student days. His attention languished, however, until 1949, when he finally attempted to paint transitions from one season to the next.

His desire to capture seasonal changes in one painting, an unprecedented aim in modern Western art, was certainly stimulated by reviewing the old sketches. But just as literary works can be invoked to help explain earlier changes, so, too, they may help account for the sudden revival of Burchfield's interest in the "all-day" paintings.

In 1949, he began to read Finnish novels, and he immersed himself in Scandinavian literature in the years immediately following. He especially admired such writers as Alexis Kivi and Sally Salminen for their remarkable descriptions of landscapes, weather conditions and seasons. He must have been particularly impressed by the correspondences he found between their observations of seasonal changes and his "all-day" sketches.

In the novels of the Norwegian, Sigrid Undset, for example, there are descriptions of the landscape that could easily have challenged and reflected Burchfield's imagination. In fact, one passage in *In the Wilderness* calls to mind his painting *The Coming of Spring*. In a few sentences, the author indicates the transition from winter to spring by describing the conditions of the ground, still covered with snow in places but already abloom with flowers in others:

> The fields that faced north still gleamed and glittered with ice, but from above on the Horse Crag water trickled and ran. And on the sunny side, across the creek, the cliff was baking. . . . Brown soil showed under the pines over there, and the thicket on the hillside toward Koerndal was hung with yellow catkins.[33]

In one of the paintings begun in 1949 and finally completed in 1960, *The Four Seasons*, Burchfield portrayed the full yearly cycle. The trees of winter at either side frame the activities of the other seasons arranged between them (color plate 40).

With a theme as broad as seasonal change, Burchfield could indulge his imagination by varying the ways in which the transitions are presented. In *The Coming of Spring* and *The Four Seasons*, nature is relatively quiescent. The facts of the changing seasons are presented in a straightforward manner. In paintings such as *Oncoming Spring*, on the other hand, he tried to show the actual process of change (color plate 35). Swirling wind forms, outlined in yellow, blow across the picture bringing renewed life to the frozen, rigid trees to the right, still held in winter's darkness. On the left, the patchy earth and partially clouded sky as well as the yellowed areas of earth indicate the loosening effects of the March winds.

Since Burchfield liked to identify himself with the month of March, one might view a painting such as *Oncoming Spring* as a self-portrait, for in its description of nature's forces and of the renewal of the landscape, and the suggestion of potential growth and the continuing processes of life, it epitomizes his aspirations as an artist. His own face, which gave him the appearance of a pleasant, mild-mannered businessman, totally masked the qualities which emerge in works such as this.

A Dream of Butterflies, *1962, watercolor, 33" x 40". Courtesy Dr. and Mrs. Theodore H. Noehren.*

MAY SONG OF THE SWAMP, *1962, watercolor, 48" x 38". Courtesy Kennedy Galleries, New York.*

SWAMP APPARITIONS, *1962, watercolor, 39 1/2" x 29 1/2". Courtesy Mrs. Donald N.C. McIntyre.*

DYING EMBERS OF AUTUMN, *1963, watercolor, 36" x 45". Courtesy Mr. and Mrs. Gordon Heald.*

FIREFLIES AND LIGHTNING, *1964—65, watercolor, 40″ x 54″. Courtesy Mr. and Mrs. George C. Berman.*

APOCALYPTIC AND NORTHERN LANDSCAPE

MOONLIGHT IN JUNE, *1961, watercolor, 45" x 33". Courtesy John D. McDonald.*

**. . . he might lie down
on the ground, then jump
up quickly to see the earth
quivering in a trembling
white light.**

IN THE LATE 1940s Burchfield became dissatisfied with the amount of detail his paintings contained. He wanted to increase even further the degree of fantasy and reduce the amount of realism by transforming the detail into what he considered pure art forms, or at least by finding an appropriate blend of realism and abstraction.

Around 1950, therefore, he began to enrich his stylistic vocabulary by lacing in great swirls of color, thick lines, indeterminate shapes, and free rather than compulsively regular caligraphic strokes. Any pretense of capturing atmospheric effects disappeared completely.

To enhance the greater freedom he now felt and required in nature's presence, he searched for new ways to perceive forms. In 1951, for instance, he wrote that he would stare at the sun for a few moments and then paint the effects this had on the images he saw. At times, he might lie down on the ground, then jump up quickly to see the earth quivering in a trembling white light. He was then fifty-eight years old!

While he was indulging himself in these near cabalistic communions, he revived the theme of the apocalyptic landscape. In its new incarnation, grass, bushes, weeds flowers, hills, and visible rays of sunlight, which often touched the earth, trembled as if in the throes of first creation. Compared with earlier versions, with their localized hillsides, the later works are celebrations of Burchfield's soul externalized. No landscapes like these ever existed except in the fancy of a lover. With the exceptions of horizon lines and occasional floral references, these works are largely nonfigurative, holding the promise of reaching object definition, but never achieving it. They invoke landscape is if it is seen in a joyous delirium. Certainly, not in the twentieth century and never before in the history of American art has an artist felt the need to project such an ecstatic vision of nature.

In these works, Burchfield does not look over a scene in the traditional manner of landscape painters, distancing himself from it. Instead, he is one with the flowers and the sun's rays. He is the wind or a petal or even a color. He is a part of the scene. In making these works, the physical and emotional toll must have been tremendous: all that passion concentrated in the end of a slender watercolor brush!

During the same years that these glorious works of affirmation were being painted, Burchfield also sifted through his feelings about the north. Continued readings in Scandanavian literature very likely helped revive his old fascination with the deep and mysterious forests he associated with that direction. In 1954, as in earlier years, he wrote of its enigmatic sway over him. He invented for it deep, water-filled gashes and lichencovered cliffs in the landscapes of his mind.

When realized on paper, they had dark and, because of their spiky forms, gothic overtones. Ultimately derived from the barren treescapes of his youth, these paintings of the north were not landscapes to wander through in enjoyment. Usually, they were winter views, and the thick, dark, leafless trees offered no hint of springtime warmth. Unlike the apocalyptic paintings, these contained deep spaces. But they were equally impenetrable

SPIRIT OF THE NORTH WOODS, *1956, watercolor, 39" x 29". Courtesy Dr. and Mrs. Robert L. Tornello.*

Noрth Woods Mood, *1956, watercolor, 40" x 33". Courtesy Sloan Galleries of American Paintings, Valparaiso University.*

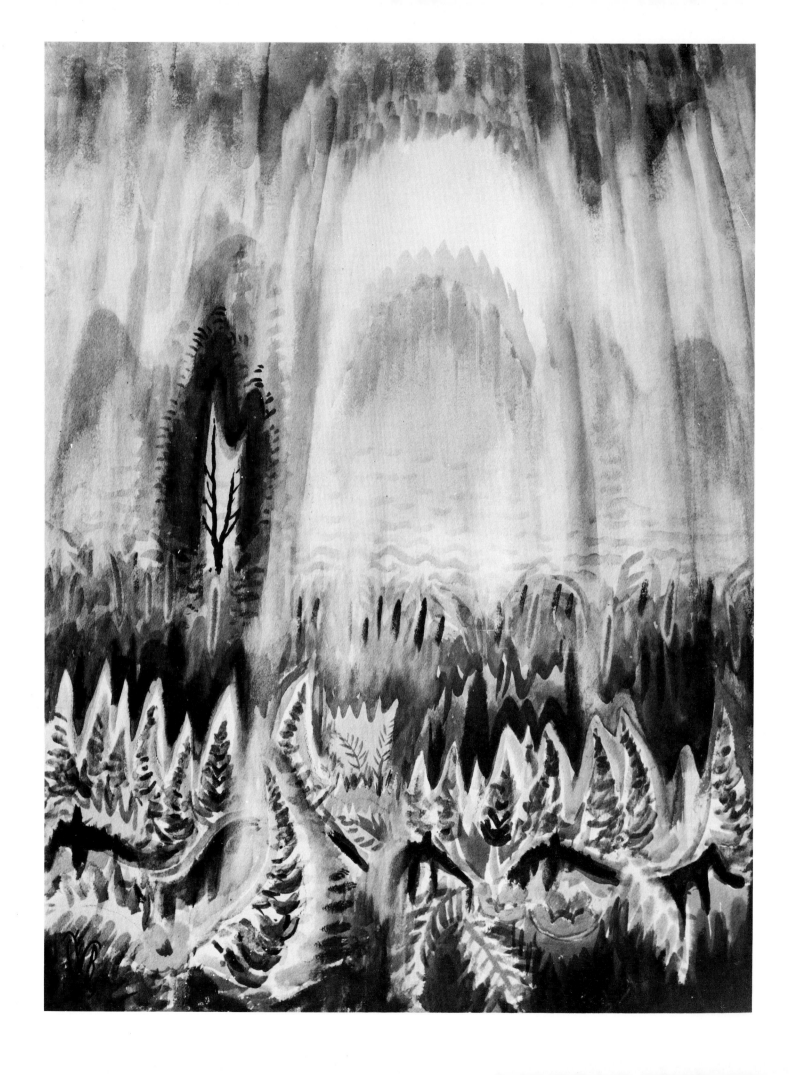

PURPLE VETCH AND BUTTERCUPS, *1959,*
watercolor, 40″ x 30″.
Courtesy Pennsylvania Academy
of the Fine Arts.

because of the forbidding aspect of the trees.

THE paintings may have served a purpose other than revealing Burchfield's fascination with the north. There appear throughout his career, views of bleak and desolate scenes. In his early works, such scenes are often populated with leafless trees presented in starkly contrasting tones. Through the middle years, factory scenes and forlorn townscapes convey a similar range of feeling. By 1950, however, Burchfield said that he had grown tired of painting rows of weatherbeaten houses, but evidently he had not lost his desire to show unpleasant weather conditions or melancholic scenes. It was the "northern" paintings that provided him with the vehicle to release those feelings associated with the earlier works. Among his late paintings, they are the only ones to suggest a hostile environment.

A qualification is necessary here. Burchfield often painted rainshowers and snowstorms, but he usually projected through them a celebration of nature's energies. One can speak of his "grand storms." But the "northern" paintings seize nature in a more purely belligerent aspect, when it offers not spectacle but enmity. Despite his overwhelming love for the landscape, Burchfield, as any forest rambler knows, also found nature an adversary worthy of respect and occasional fear.

It is this combination of celebration and respect that makes *An April Mood* (page 10) one of his richest and most allusive paintings. Begun in 1946 and reflecting the brushy textures of that period, when completed in 1955 it joined feelings suggested by the apocalyptic and the "northern" landscapes. Burchfield wanted it to express God's anger, and a "northern" scene might have sufficed if he had not wanted to suggest as well a Good Friday mood. This obviously required hints of resurrection, if not precisely in an Easter setting —a difficult task for a landscape painter. To convey the twin moods of anger and rebirth, an April storm became the appropriate backdrop. We see God's anger; we know that resurrection will follow.

THE TRIANGLE
IS CLOSED

SEPTEMBER ROAD, *1957–59, watercolor, 29 3/4" x 39 1/4". Courtesy the Burchfield Family.*

. . . from a dandelion or a cloud a whole cosmos can be invented.

AFTER 1958, because of failing health, Burchfield began to limit his activities. Asthmatic attacks and further complications limited his outdoor activities, but he still loved the eeriness of the woods at nightfall even though, increasingly, he had to enjoy it from his living room window. In letters written at this time, he expressed his great desire to be able to walk once again under a calm winter moon when the land was blanketed with snow.

At home after being hospitalized in 1957, he befriended anew the birds and trees in his backyard, particularly a young spruce, and he developed a special affection for an oak leaf that even in December had not yet blown away. It symbolized hope to him.

Yet none of his paintings alluded to his illnesses or to the frustrations of remaining indoors for such lengths of time. If anything, his work grew more frenetic and fantastic, as if each painting had become a condensation of a dozen others he might have completed had he had the strength to do so. He was given cortisone therapy in 1959 and half joked about the euphoria it worked on his mind. In truth, that year was one of his best. His stamina had returned and he completed a number of paintings begun earlier. He said that solutions became immediately apparent for every unfinished picture he took from his files.

He also began new works, and in these the line marking the side of the triangle this phase of his career represented began to reach for the starting point of the very earliest paintings. It was not just his use of fantasy, but the way he used it that became important, and it was this aspect of his work that led the way back to the beginning. In fact, one might say that there is more childhood fantasy in some works of the 1960s than in the paintings of 1915 and 1916.

Children first see and depict things individually, without regard for logical contexts. A door may appear on its side or on a roof. In a landscape, disparate forms may appear equal in size and have color intensities that obey no traditional means of suggesting depth. Flowers may loom over trees; moons may jostle suns.

In a child's way, Burchfield painted forms that grew from his inner fantasies, isolating and identifying the objects that spurred them into existence. Enormous butterflies become large leaves on a tree; a bird seem to reach up and touch the moon. Moths, flying at moonlight, grow to huge sizes; flowers and boughs defy gravity. As an old man, he understood more clearly the elements of which fantasies are made, and that from a dandelion or a cloud a whole cosmos can be invented.

HE LOOKED more acutely at his earliest paintings to help him find once again the kinds of objects he should use and the patterns they should reveal. In 1965, he said that he found himself returning often to the works of 1915, a "rhapsodic, visionary year," for inspiration. In his fiftieth year as an artist, he was literally going back to the beginning to pry further into the secrets of the human spirit.

In *Dandelion Seed Heads and the Moon,* one of Burchfield's absolute masterpieces, the cutout patterns of 1915 act as a retrospective mortar for one of his favo-

MIGRATION OF BUTTERFLIES BY MOONLIGHT, *1963, watercolor, 33" x 40". Courtesy Mr. and Mrs. Newman T. Halvorson.*

EARLY SPRING, *1966, watercolor, 38" x 43". Courtesy Charles R. Penney Collection.*

AUTUMN TO WINTER, *c. 1966, watercolor, 50" x 75". Courtesy Mr. and Mrs. Harris J. Klein.*

rite themes (color plate 44). In this version, the moon seems to exert a force on the dandelions, magically stirring them as if they were an ocean tide. The chimerical creatures, caught between the two forces, glide without effort as if suspended on moonbeams.

The insects and birds of Burchfield's earlier fancies symbolized sounds or the artist's feelings. The creatures that populate the late paintings do not seem to represent actions of this world, but of some other universe. It is as if he no longer cared to objectify his feelings in ways easily understood by others, but wanted to enter ever deeper into the world of spiritual forces. Charged with a magic light, the late paintings are the most purely imaginative he ever painted. They most clearly reflect the workings of the spirit world Burchfield sought to explore fifty years earlier. One imagines that in them he finally found what he was looking for in the view from that bedroom window of his youth.

Only as an old man, probably no longer affected by momentary exertions of nostalgia for a lost past, could he truly enter the world of fantasy and become a child again. As he steadily distilled fancy from fact, there is more than poetic truth in the thought with which he ended the essay accompanying his golden anniversary exhibition. Repeating what novelist Edna Ferber had said, he wrote: "Now, all's to do over again."[34]

NOTES

1. Many questions concerning Burchfield's life and work will be resolved when the journals, which he kept throughout his life, become available to the general public. Evidently this may not happen for a long time. They were not made available to the author during the researching and writing of this book. There are excerpts, however, on file at The Whitney Museum of American Art.

2. From excerpts of Burchfield's journals in The Whitney Museum of American Art, New York. Unless otherwise noted, subsequent references are from this source.

3. *The Summit of the Years*, by John Burroughs (Boston: Houghton Mifflin Co., 1913; and "On the Middle Border," by Charles Burchfield, *Creative Arts*, Sept., 1928.

4. *Cleveland Topics*, Nov. 24, 1917.

5. Journal, Dec. 19, 1935.

6. *Charles Burchfield*, cat. by Joseph S. Trovato (Utica: Munson-Williams-Proctor Institute, 1970).

7. *Charles Burchfield—His Golden Year*, ed. by William Steadman (Tucson: University of Arizona Press, 1965).

8. Journal, May 25, 1945.

9. *Burchfield—His Golden Year*.

10. "Charles Burchfield on Art," interview by Julian Park and W. H. Gleves, *Niagara Frontier*, Winter, 1961.

11. *Art*, by Auguste Rodin, tr. from the French of Paul Gsell by Mrs. Romilly Fedden (Boston: Small, Maynard and Co., 1912).

12. Letter to Mr. Lawrence A. Fleishman, Mr. and Mrs. Lawrence A. Fleishman Collection, Sept. 19, 1955, in Archives of American Art (microfilm).

13. Quoted in "Letters and Art," in *The Literary Digest*, Oct. 19, 1935.

14. *The New York Times*, March 7, 1920.

15. "On the Middle Border."

16. "Origins of the American Mind," by Lewis Mumford, *The American Mercury*, July, 1926.

17. *Winesburg, Ohio*, by Sherwood Anderson (New York: The Modern Library, 1919).

18. *The Ordeal of Mark Twain*, by Van Wyck Brooks (New York: E. P. Dutton and Co., Inc., 1920).

19. *Sticks and Stones*, by Lewis Mumford (New York: Boni and Liveright, 1924).

20. *Main-Travelled Roads*, by Hamlin Garland (New York: Harper and Row, 1956). First published in 1891.

21. *Main Street*, by Sinclair Lewis (New York: Harcourt, Brace and Howe, 1920).

22. *Lulu Bett*, by Zona Gale (New York: Grosset and Dunlap, 1920).

23. Lewis, *op. cit.*

24. Journal, Nov. 9, 1917, and Sept. 3, 1919.

25. Journal, Jan. 25, 1938.

26. "Hopper: Career of Silent Poetry," by Burchfield, *Art News*, March, 1950.

27. Quoted from Information Sheet, American Artists Group, Inc., Feb. 4, 1953, in Archives of American Art (microfilm).

28. *Charles Burchfield* (New York: American Artists Group, 1945).

29. Letter to Frank K. M. Rehn, Nov. 22, 1937. Courtesy of John Clancy of the Frank K. M. Rehn Galleries.

30. *Catalogue of Contemporary Paintings and Sculpture* (Buffalo: Buffalo Fine Arts Academy, Albright Art Gallery, 1949).

31. Quoted from Information Sheet, American Artists Group.

32. Letter to Mrs. Raphael Navas, Sept. 6, 1950, in Archives of American Art (microfilm).

33. *In the Wilderness*, by Sigrid Undset, tr. by Arthur G. Chater (New York: Grosset and Dunlap, 1929).

34. *Burchfield—His Golden Year*.

SELECTED BIBLIOGRAPHY

**Writings by Burchfield
listed chronologically**

"On the Middle Border," *Creative Arts* (September, 1928), xxv–xxxii.

"Norman Kent's Wood Blocks," *Print Connoisseur* (October, 1929), 313–21.

"Henry G. Keller," *American Magazine of Art* (September, 1936), 586–93.

Charles Burchfield. New York: American Artists Group, 1945.

"Hopper: Career of Silent Poetry," *Art News* (March, 1950), 14–17.

"Sun and Rocks," *Buffalo Gallery Notes* (January, 1954), 24–25.

The Drawings of Charles Burchfield, text by Charles Burchfield, edited by Edith H. Jones. New York: Praeger Publishers, 1968.

**Periodicals, Bulletins,
Catalogs, and Books listed
alphabetically by publication
or museum**

1917–29

"Painter in Water Colors," *American Art News* (October 28, 1922), 2.

"Exhibition," *The Arts* (April, 1924), 218–19.

"Exhibition," *The Arts* (April, 1926), 226–27.

Edward Hopper. "Charles Burchfield," *The Arts* (July, 1928), 5–12.

Cleveland Topics (November 24, 1917).

Henry McBride. "Burchfield," *Creative Arts* (September, 1928), xxxii.

William B. McCormick. "A Small Town in Paint," *International Studio* (March, 1925), 466–70.

"Drawings in Water Color by Charles Burchfield," Catalog, Kevorkian Gallery, New York City, 1920.

1930–39

E. M. Benson. "The American Scene," *American Magazine of Art* (February, 1934), 61, 64.

F. A. Whiting, Jr. "Note on Burchfield," *American Magazine of Art* (June, 1937), 352.

"New York Season," *Art Digest* (April 1, 1930), 16.

"New York Season," *Art Digest* (November 15, 1931), 23.

"Sad Note Creeps Into Burchfield's Art," *Art Digest* (February 15, 1934), 16.

"Critics Differ on Burchfield," *Art Digest* (March 1, 1934), 14.

"New York Criticism," *Art Digest* (November 1, 1935), 18.

"Exhibition," *Art Digest* (December 1, 1936), 18.

"Exhibition," *Art Digest* (January 1, 1939), 7.

"Charles Burchfield," *Art News* (October, 1931), 10.

"Charles Burchfield," *Art News* (February 10, 1934), 13.

"Exhibition of Paintings," *Carnegie Magazine* (March, 1938), 309–12.

"Paintings by Burchfield, Kantor and Eilshemius," *Detroit Institute of Arts Bulletin* (December, 1934), 35–36.

H. A. Read. "Charles Burchfield: A Pioneer of the New American School," *London Studio* (October, 1938), 208–11.

Charles Burchfield: Early Watercolors. New York: The Museum of Modern Art, 1930.

"On View in the New York Galleries," *Parnassus* (December, 1930), 6.

E. McCausland. "Burchfield's Water Colors, 1917–1918," *Parnassus* (December, 1939), 22.

"Charles Ephraim Burchfield," *Time* (December 24, 1934), 25.

1940–49

E. P. Richardson. "Charles Burchfield," *American Magazine of Art* (October, 1944), 208–12.

H. Furst. "Burchfield," *Apollo* (November, 1944), 5. 124–25.

"Exhibition," *Art Digest* (November 1, 1941), 7.

"Exhibition," *Art Digest* (November 1, 1943), 11.

"Explains Preference for Water Color," *Art Digest* (April 1, 1945), 56.

"Reverts Back to Early Fantasy," *Art Digest* (January 1, 1946), 9.

"Exhibition," *Art Digest* (October 15, 1947), 21.

"Burchfield's Buffalo: A Comparison Between the Artist's and the Camera's Eye," *Art News* (May 1, 1944), 13.

"Retrospective," *Cleveland Museum Bulletin* (June, 1945), 8.

Milton W. Brown. "Early Realism of Hopper and Burchfield," *College Art Journal* (No. 1, 1947), 3–11.

B. Rowland, Jr. "Burchfield's Seasons," *Fogg Museum Bulletin* (November 1946), 55–61.

R. O. Parks. "Road in Early Spring," *John Herron Institute Bulletin* (June, 1943), 16–17.

J. Abbott. "Moving Day," *Smith College Museum Bulletin* (June, 1941), 7–9.

"Paintings by Charles Burchfield," *Gallery News*, Munson-Williams-Proctor Institute (June–August, 1945), 5–6.

1950–59

"Exhibition," *Art Digest* (April 15, 1950), 10.

"Metropolitan Prospectus: Pro and Con," *Art Digest* (September, 1952), 4.

"Exhibition," *Art Digest* (November 15, 1952), 16.

B. Krase. "Charles Burchfield Profile," *Art Digest* (December 15, 1952), 9.

"Exhibition," *Art Digest* (November 15, 1954), 23.

"Throughout America: First Retrospective of Drawings and Prints," *Art News* (March, 1954), 59.

John I. H. Baur. "Burchfield's Intimate Diaries," *Art News* (January, 1956), 26–27.

John I. H. Baur. "Fantasy and Symbolism in Charles Burchfield's Early Watercolors." *Art Quarterly* (No. 1, 1956), 30–40.

L. George. "Charles Burchfield: Visit to the Artist's Studio," *Arts Magazine* (January, 1956), 26–31.

"Charles Burchfield and Morris Graves," *Boston Museum Bulletin* (1956), 295.

L. E. Prasse, "Exhibition of Drawings," *Cleveland Museum of Art Bulletin* (November, 1953), 203–04.

E. P. Richardson. "Three American Painters: Sheeler—Hopper—Burchfield," *Perspectives USA* (No. 16, 1956), 111–19.

E. Clark. "Retrospective Exhibition at Whitney Museum," *Studio International* (June, 1956), 186–87.

John I. H. Baur. *Charles Burchfield*. New York: Published for the Whitney Museum of American Art by Macmillan, 1956.

"Art From Nature," *Time* (January 23, 1956), 72–73.

1960–69

"Exhibition," *Art News* (December, 1964), 17.

"Exhibition," *Art News* (November, 1966), 11.

M. Breuning. "Burchfield's Recent Work," *Arts Magazine* (January, 1961), 50.

R. Glowacki. "Two Watercolors," *Detroit Institute of Art Bulletin* (No. 1, 1959–60), 15–16.

Julian Park and W. H. Gleves (interview). "Charles Burchfield on Art," *Niagara Frontier* (Winter, 1961), 69–80.

William E. Steadman, ed. *Charles Burchfield—His Golden Year*. Tucson: University of Arizona Press, 1965.

Since 1970

R. Downes. "Water Colorist for All Seasons," *Art News* (May, 1970), 54–57.

"Kennedy Gallery Exhibition," *Art News* (Summer, 1974), 111.

"Charles Burchfield at Frank Rehn," *Arts Magazine* (April, 1971), 81.

J. Tannenbaum. "Charles Burchfield at Kennedy," *Arts Magazine* (May, 1974), 72–73.

Charles Burchfield. Catalog by James Trovato. Utica: Munson-Williams-Proctor Institute, 1970.

INDEX

page numbers in italic indicate plates

CHARLES Burchfield was born in Ashtabula Harbor, Ohio, in 1893. Five years later, his widowed mother moved to Salem, Ohio, where he spent his childhood. He studied art at the Cleveland School of Art (now Cleveland Institute of Art) from 1912 to 1916. He then received a scholarship from the National Academy of Design in New York, where he attended classes for a single day. Between July, 1918, and January, 1919, he served in the Army and was stationed at Camp Jackson, South Carolina. He returned to Salem, but then moved to Buffalo in 1921, where he worked as a wallpaper designer for N.H. Birge and Sons until 1929. He married Bertha L. Kenreich in 1922 and they had five children. In 1925, the family moved to Gardenville, a suburb, where they lived until his death in 1967. He exhibited in New York in 1916 and 1920, and in 1924 the Montross Gallery began to handle his work. He switched to the Frank K.M. Rehn Galleries in 1929 and remained there. In 1943, he was elected a member of the National Institute of Arts and Letters. After 1949, he taught, mostly during summers, at the University of Minnesota, the Art Institute of Buffalo, the University of Buffalo, the Buffalo Fine Arts Academy, and Ohio University.

Edited by Margit Malmstrom
Designed by Bob Fillie
Set in 14 point Bodoni Book by Gerard Associates/Graphic Arts, Inc.
Printed and bound in Japan by Toppan Printing Company Ltd.